protestantism

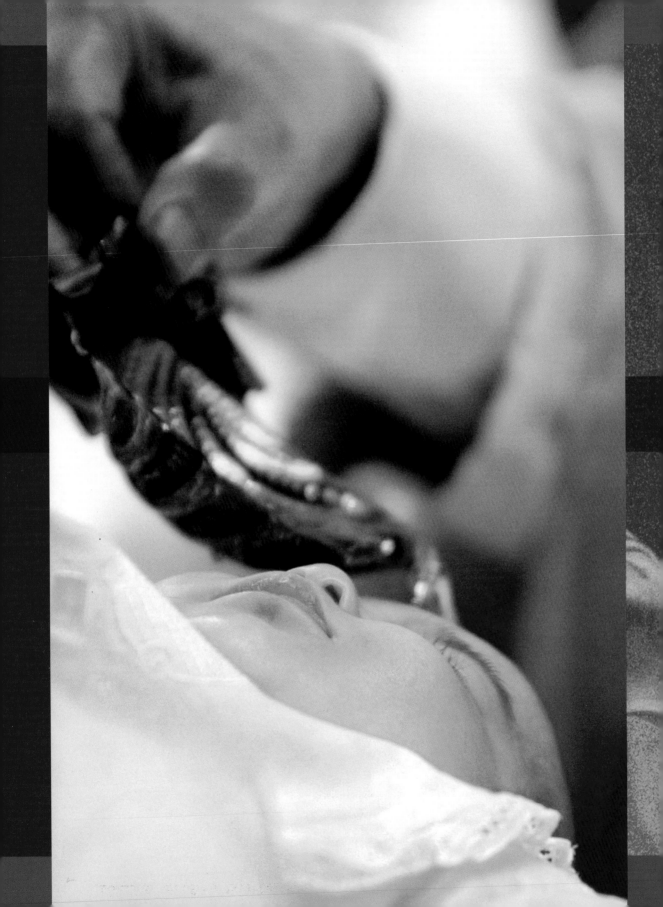

WORLD RELIGIONS

protestantism

TREVOR EPPEHIMER

Marshall Cavendish
Benchmark
New York

Marshall Cavendish Benchmark • 99 White Plains Road • Tarrytown, NY 10591-9001 • www.marshallcavendish.us
Copyright © 2007 by Marshall Cavendish Corporation • All rights reserved. No part of this book may be reproduced
or utilized in any form or by any means electronic or mechanical, including photocopying, recording, or by any in-
formation storage and retrieval system, without permission from the copyright holders. • All Internet sites were
available and accurate when the book was sent to press. • Library of Congress Cataloging-in-Publication Data •
Eppehimer, Trevor. • Protestantism / by Trevor Eppehimer. • p. cm. — (World religions) • Summary:
"Provides an overview of the history and origins, basic tenets and beliefs, organization, traditions, customs,
rites, societal and historical influences, and modern-day impact of Protestantism"—Provided by publisher.
Includes bibliographical references and index. • ISBN-13: 978-0-7614-2117-7 • ISBN-10: 0-7614-2117-3
1. Protestantism. I. Title. II. Series: World religions (Marshall Cavendish Benchmark) • BX4811.3.E67
2006280'.4—dc22 • 2005016933

Series design by Sonia Chaghatzbanian • Photo research by Candlepants, Inc. • Cover photo: Nubar
Alexanian/Corbis

The photographs in this book are used by permission and through the courtesy of: *Corbis*: Nubar Alexanian,
1, 4–5. 6–7; Reuters, 2; Rob Howard, 8; Bettmann, 55, 65, 91; Gary Houlder, 70; John Gress/Reuters, 78;
Allen T. Jules, 94; Jay Dickman, 98; Aaron Houston/*Star Ledger*, 109; Kevin Fleming, 116; Werner H. Muller,
119, back cover. *The Bridgeman Art Library*: © Galleria degli Uffizi, Florence, Italy, 15; © New-York Historical
Society, New York, USA, 58, 85. *Art Archive*: University Library Geneva/Dagli Orti, 25; University Library of
Geneva/Dagli Orti, 36; Museo del Prado, Madrid, 44–45.

Printed in China • 1 3 5 6 4 2

contents

protestantism

A man in Ethiopia reads a Bible translated into Amharic, the nation's official language. Martin Luther's eventual break with the Roman Catholic Church in the 1500s has resulted, in the twenty-first century, in the spread of a branch of faith and a set of beliefs that have been embraced throughout the world.

one

THE STORY OF MARTIN LUTHER

protestantism is best understood, along with Roman catholicism and Eastern Orthodoxy, as one of the three largest branches of Christianity. What unites these branches, and what differentiates them from the other major religious traditions, is the belief that the God of Israel, the creator of the universe, has been uniquely and definitively revealed in his son Jesus Christ and that this God exists in a Trinity, a relationship of unity among three persons (Father, Son, and Holy Spirit)—points of faith at which Christianity and Judaism part ways.

This Jesus, a Jewish man from Nazareth, preached at the beginning of the first century C.E. about a coming "Kingdom of God," a time in which God would establish a divine reign of peace and justice throughout creation. He later suffered death by crucifixion, an excruciatingly painful form of capital punishment practiced by the Roman empire at that time, outside the walls of Jerusalem. According to the Christian faith, God raised this same Jesus from the dead three days later. All three branches of Christianity also believe that Jesus will one day return to establish this Kingdom of God of which he taught and proclaimed. In the meantime, God, through the person of Jesus and by the power of the Holy Spirit, has established a human community, known as the church, which proclaims and collectively embodies the risen Jesus.

Protestantism differs from Roman Catholicism and Eastern

Orthodoxy in the way it interprets certain aspects of Christianity. It is also the youngest branch of Christianity, arising in the sixteenth century through the efforts of Martin Luther (1483–1546), a Roman Catholic priest whose theological convictions and defiant actions led to the birth of Protestant Christianity.

Martin Luther's spiritual crisis

On a summer day in July 1505, twenty-two-year-old Martin Luther, the son of simple country folk, entered the Augustinian monastery in the German town of Erfurt. His decision to join a monastery, a community of monks united by their desire to emulate Jesus in thought, word, and deed, was most likely the result of a long period of soul-searching and questioning. He would later claim that a particular dramatic event had pushed him to follow what he believed was God's call to enter into this kind of religious life. It was while traveling along a road, alone and frightened in a raging thunderstorm, that Luther, out of a deep fear that his soul was destined to spend eternity in hell, swore an oath to God that he would become a monk. Two weeks later and against his parents' wishes, especially those of his father, who had toiled hard to make sure his son received the education needed to become a lawyer, Luther made good on his oath.

Luther's life at the monastery was consumed by a painstaking regimen of intense, spiritual athleticism. Like a boxer training for the heavyweight championship or a runner preparing for a marathon, Luther was conditioning himself for what he believed was the fight of his life: the fight to save his soul.

Between one and two o'clock in the morning a loud bell roused Luther and his fellow monks from bed. In the darkness they would proceed to the church, sprinkle themselves with holy water, and kneel in prayer at the altar. There, they would begin a forty-five-minute service of prayer, ending with their chanting devotional hymns to God.

Seven times each day Luther followed this routine but he began to feel, as time wore on, that it was not rigorous enough to provide him with the spiritual cleansing he required. To supplement this routine, Luther fasted for as long as three days at a time, refusing even bread crust for nourishment. In the cold, drafty monastery, he resolved to sleep without blankets, thinking that enduring such trials would help to purify and cleanse his soul. Later, reflecting on this time as an older man, Luther admitted that if he had continued at this pace, he would have surely killed himself. As it was, the physical toll these acts took on his body would plague him in his old age in the form of bad health and frailty.

It is perhaps difficult for people of our day to comprehend the forces that drove the young Luther to such extremes. But possible parallels can be drawn to the forces that compel persons suffering from anorexia to starve themselves, those unsatisfied with their muscularity to take steroids, or those displeased with their appearance to reconfigure it through plastic surgery. Luther, perhaps like these persons, felt inadequate, unworthy, and dissatisfied with himself to the point that he felt he had to resort to drastic measures to become someone other than himself.

But the causes of Luther's self-doubt and feelings of unworthiness did not concern superficial matters like physical appearance. For Luther, the problem was rooted far deeper—in his soul. Martin Luther's dissatisfaction with himself was driving him to hate God. To him, this God to whom he had devoted his life had become a tyrant, a tormentor, and to see God in this aspect was plunging him into the throes of a profound spiritual crisis.

Luther's perception of God was, at first, like that of his fellow monks. They looked on God as a firm, but loving parent and saw themselves as God's devoted, but flawed children. Luther's view of this relationship dramatically changed after he celebrated his first

Mass. Upon performing the rite of the Eucharist, which, according to Roman Catholic doctrine, mysteriously transforms the bread and the wine on the communion table into the actual body and blood of Jesus, Luther was overcome by feelings of terror and unworthiness. Here he was, a simple priest, with what he believed was the actual body and blood of Jesus in his hands, and yet he considered himself neither holy nor righteous enough to be in such intimate proximity to the divine.

Similar feelings of unworthiness before God continued to haunt Luther. Along with his fellow monks, Luther performed regular acts of charity and confessed his sins daily—two acts that his monastic community taught made a person righteous and acceptable in God's eyes. But for Luther, no matter how often he confessed his sins or performed good works, he could not silence the inner voice that continually informed him of his unworthiness before God. From what his fellow monks could observe, Luther was the most earnest, most devoted member of their community, a monk whose constant praying and fasting revealed a degree of religious intensity that far surpassed their own. But on the inside, Luther did not feel he was growing any more pleasing in God's sight. Instead, with each passing day, he was increasingly convinced of his own unrighteousness before God. When he went to confession, he brought with him a long list of sinful thoughts and acts that he had compulsively recorded, detailing them all to the priest who would hear his confession. But each time he left fearful that he had forgotten some sins and that as a result God would never look upon him as free from sin.

In the midst of his agony, Luther came to believe that the problem that plagued him was more profound and insidious than any that could be remedied by dutifully confessing a long list of sins or saying prayers with sufficient intensity. Rather, the real cause of his spiritual suffering and mental anguish was ontological, that is, grounded in Luther's very being, in the way that he, as a human being, existed in the universe. The cause of the problem, as Luther saw it, was that as a monk he was called to live a life of holiness, moral purity, and unwavering devotion to God. But as a fallible, flawed, and therefore sinful human being, Luther doubted that it was possible to purify and cleanse one's self to the degree that God, who was infinitely holy and unendingly righteous, might consider a human being holy and righteous as well. There was a fundamental gap, Luther felt, between what he was called to do (lead a just and holy life) and who he was by virtue of his being a member of the human race (flawed and fallible), and this gap needed somehow to be bridged. But Luther felt unable to do so, despite his constant prayers, confessions, and fastings. There was nothing he could do, he believed, by his own power, to be the person he believed God wanted him to be. This dilemma, it seemed to Luther, was rendering his life an exercise in futility and was made more unbearable by his suspicion, as Luther wrote, that it was God who was behind it:

> **It is not against all natural reason that God out of his mere whim deserts men, hardens them, damns them, as if he delighted in sins and in such torments of the wretched for eternity, he who is said to be of such mercy and goodness? This appears iniquitous, cruel, and intolerable in God, by which very many have been offended in all ages. And who would not be? I was myself more than once driven to the very abyss of despair so that I wished I had never been created. Love God? I hated him!**

Luther's mentor at the Erfurt monastery, Johann von Staupitz, saw that the young monk under his care was suffering terribly and resolved to do something to remedy Luther's spiritual sickness. Knowing that Luther's state of mind was only growing worse by the day and seeing in him a tremendous work ethic and a keen intellect, Staupitz sent Luther, in 1511, to prepare to be a professor of biblical studies at the new University of Wittenburg. He knew that at the monastery Luther would never be able to heal his sick soul and thought that an extensive study of the Bible might be of great assistance to him. Luther thought it was a terrible idea and offered up every excuse he could think of to dissuade Staupitz. In the end, he relented and agreed to his mentor's wishes.

Luther's Discovery

At the University of Wittenburg, Luther plunged into his studies and was granted his doctorate in theology in 1512. His first series of lectures was on Psalms, a book in the Bible that is a collection of poetry devoted to the praise of God and of laments over human life's tribulations. It was during his preparation for his next series of lectures on Paul's letter to the Romans in the New Testament that Luther made what was, for him, a startling theological discovery.

The road to this discovery began with Luther's struggle to interpret what the apostle Paul meant in Romans 1:17 (meaning chapter one, verse seventeen) when he wrote that in the gospel, or "good news" about Jesus, "the righteousness of God is revealed through faith for faith; as it is written, 'The one who is righteous will live by faith.'" Luther did not much care for the concept of "the righteousness of God" as it only served to remind him of his own unrighteousness. And yet, in that verse, Luther understood that Paul was drawing a direct connection between the gospel concerning Jesus and God's "righteousness" or justice. How could this possibly be "good news"?

The answer, Luther believed, was to be found in Paul's quotation from the Old Testament that "The one who is righteous will live by faith." To Luther's astonishment, the source of human righteousness was not something that could be gained through acts of piety and devotion but was rather something given by God to human beings regardless of their degree of moral purity. The gap that so troubled

A portrait of reformer Martin Luther. To him, righteousness was something God granted to humans irrespective of their moral purity.

Luther between God's infinite holiness and humanity's frail and sinful state was bridged, then, not by human actions but by God's. He came to understand that faith, or trust in God, alone could make humanity righteous in God's eyes. Faith was the solution to the problem eating at his soul. Human beings could not make themselves righteous before God. Instead, it was God's gift of faith that made them righteous or "justified"; it was God who had to overcome the gap, not humanity. Reflecting on this discovery, Luther wrote the following:

> Though I lived as a monk without reproach, I felt that I was a sinner before God with an extremely disturbed conscience. . . . I did not love, yes, I hated the righteous God who punishes sinners, and secretly. . . . I was angry with God. . . . Thus I raged with a fierce and troubled conscience. Nevertheless, I beat importunately upon Paul at that place [Romans 1:17], most ardently desiring to know what St. Paul wanted.

> At last, by the mercy of God, meditating day and night, I gave heed to the context of the words, namely, "In it the righteousness of God is revealed, as it is written, 'He who through faith is righteous shall live.'" There I began to understand that the righteousness of God is that by which the righteous lives by a gift of God, namely by faith. . . . Here I felt that I was altogether born again and had entered paradise itself through open gates.

At last, Luther had resolved his spiritual crisis as his mentor at Erfurt had hoped through intensive biblical study. Luther's discovery in Paul's letter to the Romans—something that would later become known as the doctrine of justification by faith alone—eventually became the theological cornerstone of the Protestant Reformation and one of the most important theological principles of Protestantism.

corruption in the church

Outside Luther's personal struggles and theological discoveries, the Roman Catholic Church at that time was in a weakened state. It was the role of the papacy, or the office of the pope, to guide and govern the Catholic Church. In the years 1378–1417, the papacy experienced the Great Schism of the West, a time when two different persons claimed the title of pope. Although this matter was resolved, these and other events caused some faithful Christians to grow cynical of the papacy, especially as it became increasingly intertwined with Europe's monarchies. Sporadic discoveries of corruption within the church hierarchy further compounded the cynicism among some Christians.

The most blatant instances of Church corruption stemmed from the activity of the parish clergy. While some clergy honored their vows and performed their priestly tasks with integrity, a culture of corruption festered among the ordained. All of the Church's clergy at the time took a vow of celibacy, but a significant number broke this vow, fathering children without even attempting to conceal it from their parishioners. Monasteries that had been established as centers of simple living and prayerful activity were increasingly becoming centers of expensive tastes and leisure activities. In addition, the educational requirements for monastic life, whose high standards had produced some of Europe's great philosophical theologians, were eased and the once stimulating intellectual environment quickly dimmed. As for the parish clergy, only minimal educational training was required for an appointment, resulting in a slew of ignorant clergy delivering embarrassingly uninformed sermons to their parishioners. None of this was lost on the people in the pews, whose confidence in their Church and its leaders was steadily eroding.

The pope of Luther's day, Leo X (1475–1521), was determined to reverse the Church's decline and to stamp his tenure in the papacy with a lasting mark. He resolved that the magnificent Basilica of Saint Peter in Rome, a project begun by the previous pope, Julius II, would be completed during his reign. To complete the basilica would be expensive and incur costs that, by all projections, would greatly exceed the church's revenues.

Just like the head of any other large organization in need of money, Leo, along with his advisors, devised a fund-raising campaign to pay for the completion of Saint Peter's. The idea they came up with was the sale of indulgences.

The sale of indulgences

Indulgences were certificates, purchased either for one's self or on behalf of a departed loved one, that would guarantee absolution (forgiveness for sins) on the authority of Pope Leo. In the case of the departed, these indulgences were thought to be effective in releasing the soul from purgatory. It is a realm, according to Roman Catholic teaching, where those whose sins were grave enough to keep them out of heaven, but not serious enough to merit hell, went for purification. Pope Leo and his advisors thought that the revenue generated by the sale of indulgences might go a long way toward ensuring the speedy completion of Saint Peter's.

The person assigned to coordinate indulgence sales in Germany was a Dominican priest named Johann Tetzel (about 1465–1519). Tetzel was a master marketer and a savvy businessman whose zeal for selling indulgences led him to take liberties with Christian doctrine. For example, Tetzel claimed that buying an indulgence would be more effective than the rite of baptism in cleansing one's soul. He even coined a catchy phrase that he hoped would spur sales: "As soon as the coin in the coffer rings, the soul from purgatory springs."

Meanwhile, Martin Luther was busy lecturing on and instructing others in the notion of justification by faith alone that he had discovered in his study of Romans. While Luther's discussion of this topic roused some academic interest among students and faculty at the University of Wittenburg, his conviction that it represented a completely new way of understanding the gospel failed to make the kind of impression for which he had hoped. But when his theological convictions collided with Tetzel's marketing campaign, their revolutionary nature came to light.

"Here I stand"

In addition to his teaching duties at the university, Luther pastored a local congregation and became aware of Tetzel's activities when he heard that parishioners had spent their wages on papal indulgences. Luther, like many other educated Germans, was outraged at Tetzel's sales tactics, but instead of ignoring them, as others did, he resolved to take action.

For Luther, the issue of indulgence sales was far more serious than the instances of priests not adhering to their vows. At stake, he felt, was the integrity of the gospel, the heart of the Christian faith itself, for if what he discovered in Paul's letter to the Romans was true—that only faith, and not works, made human beings righteous in God's eyes—then the pope's teaching that one could increase one's righteousness by purchasing indulgences stood in contradiction to that gospel. Resolved to make a stand for the very beliefs to which he had devoted his life, Luther performed the act that, in retrospect, marked the birth of Protestant Christianity.

On the eve of All Saints Day—October 31, 1517—Luther nailed Ninety-five Theses to the doors of the Castle Church in Wittenberg for the town to read. This was a common practice at the time used by those people wishing to make their views known. The Ninety-five Theses were similar to earlier writings Luther had circulated within the university, but these were tailored specifically to address the issue of indulgence sales. Here, for example, are nine of those ninety-five:

43. Christians are to be taught that he who gives to the poor or lends to the needy does a better deed than he who buys indulgences.

50. Christians are to be taught that if the pope knew the exactions of the indulgence preachers, he would rather that the basilica of St. Peter were burned to ashes than built up with the skin, flesh, and bones of his sheep.

62. The true treasure of the church is the most holy gospel of the glory and grace of God.

63. But this treasure is naturally most odious [to the wealthy], for it makes the first to be last [Matthew 20:16].

64. On the other hand, the treasure of indulgences is naturally most acceptable [to the wealthy], for it makes the last to be first.

81. This unbridled preaching of indulgences makes it difficult even for learned men to rescue the reverence which is due the pope from slander or from the shrewd questions of the laity,

82. Why does not the pope empty purgatory for the sake of holy love and the dire need of the souls that are there . . . [than] for the sake of miserable money with which to build a church?

86. Why does not the pope . . . build this one basilica of St. Peter with his own money rather than with the money of poor believers?"

90. To repress these very sharp arguments of the laity by force alone, and not to resolve them by giving reasons, is to expose the church and the pope to the ridicule of their enemies and to make Christians unhappy.

As is apparent in thesis 50, Luther, while aggressively seeking to discredit the theological rationale behind indulgence sales, felt himself to be a defender of the pope and the pope's integrity among lay Christians. Yet, as he would soon discover, Pope Leo did not see it that way.

The Ninety-five Theses were rapidly distributed among the regional population, thanks to the recent invention of the moveable-type printing press. A copy eventually landed in the hands of Pope Leo, sent by a member of the German nobility. Outraged by what he perceived to be an attempt by a clever monk to undermine his financial campaign, Leo, working through Emperor Maximilian of the Holy Roman empire, arranged for Luther to appear before an audience in Augsburg that included Cardinal Cajetan (1480–1547), one of the Vatican's sharpest theological minds. Cajetan was instructed to meet this university professor who was calling indulgence sales into question and to extract from him a repudiation of his Ninety-five Theses.

The prince who ruled Luther's region, Frederick the Wise (1463–1525), who privately was a great admirer of Luther and his Ninety-five Theses, was concerned for Luther's safety (the punishment for those considered "heretics" was to be burned alive at the stake) and secured from Maximilian a promise that Luther would not be harmed.

Still, by traveling to face an assembly that included his country's rulers, Cardinal Cajetan, and other members of the Church hierarchy, Luther was aware that he was risking his life.

Luther's face-to-face encounter with Cajetan at Augsburg did little to resolve the conflict between Luther's theological principles and the sale of indulgences. Luther, in fact, was not permitted to speak or address the assembly in any way. Instead, Cajetan, as instructed, insisted that Luther recant, or take back, everything that he had written in his Ninety-five Theses. After realizing that there would be no opportunity to discuss his ideas and defend his document before the cardinal, and then discovering that there was a good chance he would be arrested and taken into custody, Luther departed in the middle of the night for Nürnberg before action could be taken against him. He arrived back in Wittenberg soon after.

Luther's standing with Rome took an even sharper turn for the worse following a public debate with John Eck (1486–1543), a professor at the nearby University of Ingolstadt who sided with Pope Leo against Luther. During the debate, which took place in the town of Leipzig, Eck was successful in getting Luther to admit that the Bible was a greater authority in matters pertaining to the Christian faith than was the pope. While such a stance would later become a staple of Protestant theology and would raise few eyebrows today, professing such a view at that time was a serious theological offense. Soon after, Pope Leo drafted the document *Exsurge Domine*, a formal condemnation of Luther and his teachings, in which Luther was likened to a wild boar wreaking havoc in the Lord's vineyard. *Exsurge Domine* also ordered that all books, pamphlets, and published lectures by Luther be burned. Leo, however, gave Luther one last chance to avoid excommunication, that is, his forced removal from the Church, by granting him sixty days to recant his teaching and resubmit himself to the authority of the Vatican. Outraged by the tactics employed against him, Luther publicly burned the copy of

Exsurge Domine that was delivered to him and declared that he would continue to speak out against the sale of indulgences and to defend his belief that the sum of the gospel was justification by faith alone.

The final confrontation between Luther and his opponents took place on April 16, 1521, this time in the town of Worms. There, Luther appeared before Charles V, the Holy Roman emperor who had succeeded Maximilian and was a supporter of Pope Leo.

Laid out before Luther when he arrived were copies of his books and essays. After confirming that these were his writings, Luther was asked whether he cared to reject some of them and, if so, to identify which ones. After requesting some time alone to think it over, Luther returned to appear before the audience that anxiously awaited his response. The emperor's interrogator again asked him, "Do you or do you not repudiate your books and the errors which they contain?"

Standing firm, Luther uttered the response that would split the Western church in two, with Protestants on one side and Catholics on the other: "Unless I am convicted by Scripture and plain reason—I do not accept the authority of popes and councils, for they have contradicted each other—my conscience is captive to the Word of God. I cannot and I will not recant anything, for to go against conscience is neither right nor safe. Here I stand, I cannot do otherwise. God help me. Amen."

The final edict from Worms, issued by Charles V, stated: "Luther is to be regarded as a convicted heretic. . . . No one is to harbor him. His followers are also to be condemned. His books are to be eradicated from the memory of man."

The Fallout

What took place that day at Worms would forever change not only the Church but also European society and politics. For Luther, his rebellion against the Vatican was a matter of theological principle, for the integrity of the gospel, in his view, was the main issue at stake. For others, the significance of Luther's defiance resided outside theology. Some members of the German ruling class saw Luther as a courageous symbol of German nationalism asserted against a Church that was increasingly controlled by southern European bishops and cardinals whose decisions often benefited their home countries at the expense of the rest of Europe. For them, Luther's stand was an opportunity to assert German independence from the Vatican, thus granting the local nobility more power in regional affairs.

Another response came from German peasants who, under the feudal system, worked the fields of the nobility for little pay. Many of them saw in Luther's declaration that Christians were to submit only to the authority of scripture and not to the rule of men, an opportunity to revolt against the nobility. Inspired in part by Luther's teachings, Thomas Müntzer led the bloody—and unsuccessful— Peasants' War (1524–1525) that ended, by many accounts, in more than one hundred thousand deaths. Luther, in an essay entitled "Secular Authority," argued against Müntzer, saying that Christians were to obey the laws and authority of those who governed them and that God's authority only pertained to spiritual matters. He called this the Two Kingdoms theory of government—one kingdom was God's, the other was that of human rulers, and the division of powers should not be confused.

The effect on the Western Church was a dramatic split between those who sided with Luther and those who opted to remain loyal to papal authority as before. These two groups would later be identified as Protestants and Catholics, respectively.

Luther never intended to establish his own theological movement nor a Church separate from the Roman Catholic Church. Nevertheless, political events and theological controversies made such a split inevitable. Other Reformation movements soon followed: Huldrych Zwingli's in Switzerland; John Calvin's, which started in France and

Swiss reformer Huldrych Zwingli believed there was a difference between the word of God as proclaimed by a pastor or preacher and "the internal word of God," the ways in which God was revealed to be present in the human heart.

relocated to Geneva; King Henry VIII's in England, which began after the pope refused to grant the king a divorce; and the Anabaptist or Radical Reformation movement, which advocated that Christians form separate societies free from the influence of governments or principalities. Martin Luther, however, is widely regarded as the founder of Protestantism, the Augustinian monk from humble origins whose initial spiritual crisis became the epicenter of a social, political, and theological earthquake that affected the Western world in ways that are still being felt.

two

PROTESTANT THEOLOGY

protestantism is marked by profound and complex theological principles. This is especially true of what is called classical Protestantism. Classical Protestant theology was developed by Martin Luther and John Calvin (1509–1564). Calvin wrote what many people consider to be the greatest theological work of the Reformation period, *Institutes of the Christian Religion.* In the *Institutes* he discusses in great detail the important theological topics of Christianity from a Protestant perspective.

The theology of classical Protestantism is different from that of "Arminian Protestantism," named for Jacobus Arminius (1560–1609), a Dutch theologian whose understanding of how human beings come to be "saved" broke with that of Luther and Calvin.

classical protestantism

The Authority of Scripture: *Sola Scriptura*

All religions have a center of authority from which their leaders organize and direct the lives of the religion's practitioners. Before Luther's revolt, Western Christianity looked to the papacy as that center of authority. It was the pope who would settle disputes, clarify points of doctrine, and guide the church in its ongoing effort to interpret the Bible. But after the Protestants established a form of Christianity that no longer took its lead from the pope, a lack of central authority prevailed, a state that had to be altered if Protestantism was to avoid becoming a cult of personality. The early Protestants believed that the new center of authority was to be found in the Bible itself. *Sola scriptura*, a Latin term that means "only scripture," and not the pope, thus became the early Protestants' motto, a profession that the Bible was their highest authority.

The problem, however, was that at the time of the Protestant Reformation the Bible had not yet been translated into the languages that everyday Europeans spoke. Its reading and interpretation fell to literate clergy who were capable of deciphering the Hebrew and Greek texts and their Latin translation, which was known as the Vulgate. It was Luther's and the other reformers' deep conviction that the laity, the average people in the pews, should have unmediated access to the Bible—should, that is, be able to read it for themselves without the clergy telling them how it should be interpreted. For this reason, one of the first projects Luther started, following his official break from Rome, was a translation of the Bible into German. Luther hoped that his translation would provide literate Germans with the opportunity to read scripture in their own language.

Perhaps one of the most important theological components of the *sola scriptura* doctrine was the Reformation belief that the Holy Spirit (what the Christian doctrine of the Trinity teaches is the third person, or manifestation, of the one God) secretly works in the heart of the person of faith to enable that individual to interpret the Bible correctly. According to John Calvin, only when the Holy Spirit works within the heart of the person reading or hearing the Bible does the Bible become capable of revealing the nature of God's character to that person:

> **Since for unbelieving men religion seems to stand by opinion alone, they, in order not to believe anything foolishly or lightly, both wish and demand rational proof. . . . But I reply:**

the testimony of the Spirit is more excellent than all reason. For as God alone is a fit witness of himself in his Word, so also the Word will not find acceptance in men's hearts before it is sealed by the inward testimony of the Spirit. The same Spirit, therefore, who has spoken through the mouths of the prophets must penetrate into our hearts to persuade us that they faithfully proclaimed what had been divinely commanded.

Somewhat idealistically the early reformers thought that the principle of *sola scriptura* would allow Protestants to return to an authentic form of Christianity, one that had not been seen or experienced since the time of Christianity's origins and that the theological disagreements and controversies, which had long been a part of the church's existence, would dissipate soon after. As would become apparent, it was not quite that easy to establish a theological consensus among Protestants by way of *sola scriptura*. Once the Bible was translated into different languages, many different ways of understanding it surfaced. With no central authority in place to determine which interpretation was to be preferred, Protestantism split into many different denominational forms, evidenced today by the existence of a plurality of Protestant churches—Lutheran, Presbyterian, Methodist, Episcopal, Baptist, and Pentecostal, for example.

Although the Protestant principle of *sola scriptura* did not produce a theological consensus, what it did do was encourage non-ordained Christians to encounter the scriptures directly, without the assistance of a cleric. This then became a basis for the Protestant notion of the "priesthood of all believers," a concept that denoted the equality of the ordained and the laity before the final authority of the Bible. *Sola scriptura* also functioned as a check against the potential abuse of clerical power by making it possible for the laity to gauge clerical teaching against the Bible—something that had not been possible when only the ordained could read it.

Justification by Faith Alone

A second important component of Protestant theology is the doctrine of justification by faith alone. This doctrine is primarily concerned with the question of salvation, that is, how Christians should understand the conditions under which human beings come to be "saved," or placed in right relationship with God.

According to traditional Christian teaching, a breach or a rupture between human beings and God occurred following the Fall of Adam and Eve (the story told in the third chapter of Genesis). The condition caused by this breach became known as original sin, whose existence, it was taught, is not only present in all of humanity but also places a significant obstacle to humanity's ability to know and love God properly. All Christian teachings concerning salvation give some account as to how this obstacle is removed or overcome.

Historically, Christian debates concerning the proper understanding of salvation revolved around the question of whose job it was to overcome the obstacles to right relations between God and human beings: God's, humanity's, or some combination of the two. The Catholic Church at the time of the Reformation taught, and continues to teach, that salvation involves God and humanity working together to overcome the effects of original sin. From one side of the breach, God does God's part by taking on human form in Jesus, dying on the cross for the sins of humanity, and offering all those who believe in Jesus eternal salvation, provided that one chooses of one's own free will to believe in Jesus, participate in the life of the church, and perform acts of love and mercy in accordance with Jesus's teachings. This understanding was the source of Luther's spiritual crisis in the monastery.

Luther, in his study of Paul's letter to the Romans, felt that he had come upon a different understanding of salvation. This understanding held that there were no conditions placed on God's gift of salvation or what is often referred to as God's grace. In contrast to the Catholic view, Luther believed that God's grace was a free gift: nothing was required of the one who received it. Humans needed to do no prior work to receive it nor perform good works to keep the gift. It was God's responsibility, not humanity's, to overcome the breach caused by original sin and to set right the relationship between God and humanity that had fallen off track.

In arguing for this position, the reformers cited, in addition to the letter to the Romans, the following passage from the letter to the Ephesians: "For by grace you have been saved through faith, and this is not your own doing; it is the free gift of God—not the result of works, so that no one may boast." (Ephesians 2:8–9) Catholic theologians described their position as the doctrine of justification by faith formed by love, that is, by a faith made effective through rightly oriented human activity, and cited this New Testament passage from the Letter of James in response:

> **What good is it, my brothers and sisters, if you say you have faith but do not have works? Can faith save you? If a brother or sister is naked and lacks daily food, and one of you says to them, "Go in peace; keep warm and eat your fill," and yet you do not supply their bodily needs, what is the good of that? So faith by itself, if it has no works, is dead. (James 2:14–17)**

Protestants were sensitive to the charge that their doctrine of justification by faith alone could lead to the kind of moral and ethical irresponsibility described in the letter of James. That is, the question Protestants often find themselves having to answer is that if it is the case that one is saved by a faith that is freely given by God, irrespective of human works, then is the Christian free to sit back, enjoy the gift of salvation, and go on an extended ethical vacation? Does Protestantism, by this teaching, encourage morally lax behavior?

In response to such objections, Luther wrote the following in one of his most famous treatises, "The Freedom of the Christian":

> **Although the Christian is thus free from all works, he . . . ought to think: "Although I am an unworthy and condemned man, my God has given me in Christ all the riches of righteousness and salvation without any merit on my part, out of pure, free mercy, so that from now on I need nothing except faith which believes that this is true. Why should I not therefore freely, joyfully, with all my heart, and with an eager will do all things which I know are pleasing and acceptable to such a Father who has overwhelmed me with his inestimable riches? I will therefore give myself as a Christ to my neighbor, just as Christ offered himself to me. . . ."**

Luther argued that people who have experienced the gift of salvation, given freely by God without regard to whether they were deserving of it, will, out of gratitude for this gift, spontaneously perform the works of love, mercy, and charity to which they are called as Christians. This does not mean that questions of ethics and morals are to be excluded from one's understanding of the Christian life, but only that they are always the *second* consideration and should be thought of as that which follows or flows from the free gift of salvation, not something that somehow makes salvation possible. As Luther wrote in that same essay: "Our faith in Christ does not free us from works but from false opinions concerning works, that is, from the foolish presumption that justification is acquired by works." Or, as the Letter to the Ephesians states it, people are saved, not by good works, but for good works. (Ephesians 2:10)

Predestination and the "Invisible" Church

Another question raised by the Protestant doctrine of justification by faith alone is whether faith itself could be conceived of as a kind of work. Was faith something that a human being could choose to have or did faith have to be given by God as a gift? If one answered that faith was something that human beings had the ability to choose of their own free will, then this would seem to violate the notion of justification by faith alone, as the act of faith itself would be a precondition for salvation and, therefore, a "work." But if one answered that faith itself was a gift from God, this potentially suggested that God "played favorites," that God opted to give the gift of faith to some and not to others. This, then, presented the early reformers with a theological dilemma that needed to be resolved.

Both Luther and Calvin agreed that the doctrine of justification by faith alone was the essential theological teaching of the Reformation and that it should serve as the guiding principle by which they would solve all subsequent theological disputes. For this reason, both insisted that to preserve the integrity of the doctrine of justification by faith alone, it should be taught that faith itself was a gift from God and not something that resulted from human choice. This ensured that salvation would be, without exception, a gift from God that was free from the taint of "works righteousness," which the reformers associated with Catholic theology. The reformers taught that God gave humanity both faith, as the means to salvation, and the power or inclination to choose it. As Luther wrote in the treatise "The Bondage of the Will":

> **I frankly confess that, for myself, even if it could be, I should not want "free-will" to be given me, nor anything to be left**

in my own hands to enable me to endeavour after salvation; not merely because in face of so many dangers, and adversities, and assaults of devils, I could not stand my ground and hold fast my "free will" (for one devil is stronger than all men, and on these terms no man could be saved); but because, even were there no dangers, adversities, or devils, I should still be forced to labour with no guarantee of success, and to beat my fists at the air. If I lived and worked to all eternity, my conscience would never reach comfortable certainty as to how much it must do to satisfy God. Whatever work I had done, there would still be a nagging doubt as to whether it pleased God, or whether He required something more. The experience of all who seek righteousness by works proves that; and I learned it well enough myself over a period of many years, to my own great hurt. But now that God has taken my salvation out of the control of my own will, and put it under the control of His, and promised to save me, not according to my working or running, but according to His own grace and mercy, I have the comfortable certainty that He is faithful and will not lie to me, and that He is also great and powerful, so that no devils or opposition can break Him or pluck me from Him. . . . Thus it is that, if not all, yet some, indeed many, are saved; whereas, by the power of "free will" none at all could be saved, but every one of us would perish.

Luther's argument against human "free will" with respect to salvation is that it would be irresponsible of God to allow human beings that much freedom, especially in a matter like salvation. If people were left to act of their own free will, Luther believed that humanity, on account of original sin which made humanity consistently prone to temptation and bad decision-making, would always choose against God and the life of faith. Knowing this, God took the matter of salvation out of human hands altogether.

And yet, this raised another particularly thorny theological issue for classical Protestant theology concerning hell, the realm where, according to traditional Christian teaching, the souls of unsaved persons go after death. In a number of New Testament passages, most notably Matthew 25:31–46, it is suggested that on an upcoming day of judgment, people will be separated just "as a shepherd separates the sheep from the goats" (Matthew 25:32), and that those who refused to care for the hungry, the sick, and the poor "will go away into eternal punishment, but the righteous into eternal life." (Matthew 25:46) The crucial theological question for the reformers became this: If it was true that human beings did not choose the life of faith of their own free will, but that it was a gift from God, was it also true that God gave this gift only to certain people and therefore condemned those to whom the gift was not given to the place described in Matthew 25, commonly referred to as hell?

Constrained by the logic of the central doctrine of the Reformation, the doctrine of justification by faith alone, and what the reformers perceived to be the clear and unmistakable New Testament references to the existence of a place of eternal punishment, Protestant theology answered that, yes, it seemed to be the case that God predestined some to whom faith, and thus eternal salvation, would be given. For others the gift of faith would not be extended. This became known as the doctrine of double predestination, a teaching that was developed and explicated most notably by John Calvin in his *Institutes of the Christian Religion*:

> **In actual fact, the covenant of life [the Gospel] is not preached equally among all men, and among those to whom it is preached, it does not gain the same acceptance. . . . In**

John Calvin introduced the tenets
of the Reformation to his home
base in Switzerland. Through
the years, Calvinist churches,
which followed a strict moral
code, established a presence
in Geneva, Switzerland; Great
Britain; the United States; France
and Hungary, where they became
a visible and vocal minority; and
the Netherlands and parts of
Germany, where they became the
dominant Protestant group.

> this diversity the wonderful depth of God's judgment is made known. For there is no doubt that this variety also serves the decision of God's eternal election. If it is plain that it comes to pass by God's bidding that salvation is freely offered to some while others are barred from access to it, at once great and difficult questions spring up. . . . A baffling question this seems to many. For they think nothing more inconsistent than that out of the common multitude of men some should be predestined to salvation, others to destruction. . . . [But we] shall never be clearly persuaded, as we ought to be, that our salvation flows from the wellspring of God's free mercy until we come to know his eternal election, which illumines God's grace by this contrast: that he does not indiscriminately adopt all into the hope of salvation but gives to some what he denies to others.

Elsewhere, Calvin referred to the doctrine of double predestination as the *decretum horribile*, a Latin term meaning "horrible decree," an indication that Calvin himself knew that this aspect of Protestant thought was not its most attractive. It was unclear to Calvin why God would choose some people to receive salvation and others not, but he thought that ultimately human beings should not speculate on the reasons for this and instead leave all issues regarding human salvation to God whose mysterious ways and infinite wisdom were far beyond anything the human mind could comprehend.

One thing the Protestant emphasis on predestination accomplished was solving for the reformers a problem with which they had been struggling following the break from the authority of the pope, namely, the development of a Protestant theological understanding of the church, which the pope's theologians had accused the reformers of unnecessarily tearing apart. It is perhaps difficult for people today to understand the full significance of this division as political parties, business entities, and community organizations often split apart because of various controversies, misunderstandings, and disagreements. The difference between these modern schisms and the church is that the latter is commonly held in Christian teaching to constitute the mystical "body of Christ" on earth. The group of Christians who gather together to pray, worship, and serve the needs of their surrounding communities is believed to be the collective, mysterious embodiment of the resurrected Jesus. Given this understanding of the church, Catholic critics claimed that the reformers had committed one of the greatest sins imaginable—tearing Jesus in two through the division they had brought to the Christian church.

To refute this charge, Calvin employed the doctrine of predestination to make a distinction between what he called the "visible" and the "invisible" church. The visible church, Calvin contended, is the church that one experiences with the senses: it is located in a particular place, on a particular corner, and is composed of one's friends and neighbors with whom one can pray, join hands, sing hymns, and study scripture. The visible church is the Christian community that exists in the same time and space as we ourselves exist, such that one can point it out to another person and say, "Look, *there* it is. That's where I go to church."

The invisible church, on the other hand, is not immediately detectable by way of the physical senses. It is composed only of those people who are elected, or predestined, to share eternity with God in heaven. Calvin explained that because such persons were known only to God and not to other human beings, the existence of the invisible church was not something people could point to or experience with their physical senses. By making this distinction between the visible and the invisible church, Calvin and the other reformers felt they had refuted the charge that they had torn apart the body of Jesus. Only the invisible church, they claimed, could be perfectly equated with that body. So, while the Reformation may have torn apart the visible church, the invisible church remained intact:

> . . . to embrace the unity of the church in this way, we need not see the church with the eyes or touch it with the hands. Rather, the fact that it belongs to the realm of faith should warn us to regard it no less since it passes our understanding than if it were clearly visible. And our faith is no worse because it recognizes a church beyond our ken [our understanding]. For here we are not bidden to distinguish between reprobate [those not given the gift of faith] and elect [those to whom it has been given]—that is for God alone, not for us, to do . . . .

Calvin did attempt to make some provisions with respect to double predestination and the invisible church to guard against potential abuses. First, he contended that it was impossible for any human being to determine which people had been elected by God to receive salvation and which had not. Such things were known only to God and were therefore beyond the capacity of human beings to know. Therefore, Calvin believed, human beings had no right to judge or condemn one another nor to determine who belonged to the invisible church and who did not. Second, Calvin strongly believed that the doctrine of double predestination should never be preached or proclaimed in such a way as to cause anyone to lose hope. On this matter, Calvin often cited the fourth-century theologian Augustine: "For as we know not who belongs to the number of the predestined or who does not belong, we ought to be so minded as to wish that all men be saved." Third, Calvin wrote that Christians should never turn their backs on the visible church, for while he believed that it

These communion trays are filled with cubed bread and glasses of grape juice. John Calvin saw communion as a vital element of and link to the workings of the visible church.

could not be equated with the body of Jesus, it was also true that participation in the visible church was essential to the life of the Christian as it provided the instruction, training, and discipline necessary to live the life of faith. In addition, Calvin maintained that whenever the sacraments of communion and baptism were properly administered and the Word of God rightly preached and heard in the visible church, then "it is not to be doubted, a church of God exists." Calvin emphasized these points so that Protestants would maintain contact with and participate regularly in the visible church.

Despite Calvin's warnings, the doctrine of double predestination was applied in precisely the ways in which he demanded that it not be. Subsequent generations of Calvinists believed that they were capable of determining who was among the elect and who was not. Some Calvinist preachers also made the "horrible decree" the subject of fearsome sermons that were designed to strike terror in the hearts of their congregations. It was in response to such abuses that what is called Arminian Protestant theology was developed.

Arminian protestantism: faith and free will

Like the classical Protestantism of Luther and Calvin, Arminian Protestantism held fast to the *sola scriptura* doctrine, believed in the concept of the "priesthood of all believers," and did not look to the pope as a privileged authority in matters of faith and doctrine. It also believed in the doctrine of justification by faith alone but understood this doctrine differently from classical Protestantism.

Arminian Protestantism receives its name from Jacobus Arminius, the Dutch theologian who disagreed with Luther and Calvin on the issue of the role of human free will in a proper Christian understanding of salvation, or how it is that Christians believe human beings come to be "saved" in Jesus. Arminius rejected classical Protestantism's doctrines of unconditional justification and predestination, the notion that human beings play no active role in their salvation. Arminius taught that faith was offered to all of humanity through Jesus, but that God granted individuals the freedom to accept or reject this offer. In Arminius's view, God was more compassionate, more just, and less arbitrary than depicted by the classical Protestant doctrine of predestination.

Thus, the defining feature of Arminian Protestantism was the separation of the doctrine of justification by faith alone, which it accepted, from the Calvinist doctrine of predestination, which it rejected. Arminians taught that God's offer of salvation through faith is to be thought of as an invitation to all of humanity, not only to a selected few. It is the responsibility of human beings, according to Arminius, to take advantage of this offer by using the freedom that God grants to accept the gift of faith and be saved. This means that human beings have the option of rejecting the offer of salvation as well. In Arminian Protestantism, human beings had a more active role to play in their own salvation than in Classical Protestantism.

Luther believed that the responsibility to make a choice for or against faith was too great for a human being to assume on his own. From Luther's standpoint, this would be like asking someone who had never taken flying lessons to land a 747, but worse, for this matter pertained to one's eternal destiny. But from the Arminian vantage, the more fitting analogy would be that of a person hearing a knock at the door and deciding whether to answer. Arminians felt that at some point in everyone's life, God, in the person of Jesus Christ, would "knock" on the heart of the human being, asking to come in. It was up to the individual to decide whether to let God in. For this reason, Arminian Protestants have been very active in evangelism, or the spreading of the gospel among non-Christians so as to convert them to Christianity, especially in parts of the world where other religions are dominant.

This issue of the role of free will in the Christian understanding of salvation continues to divide Protestants, with Lutherans and Calvinists falling on the classical Protestant side, and Methodists, Baptists, Pentecostals, and contemporary, nondenominational evangelicals on the Arminian one.

three

MAJOR PROTESTANT
MOVEMENTS

It is difficult to give an account of the organization and structure of Protestantism. As hard as one may try to give Protestantism a coherent shape and to divide it into categories, there are a few movements that defy such attempts. The diversity within Protestantism is due, to a large extent, to the fact that with only the Bible as its central governing authority, Protestantism developed a wide variety of denominations, movements, and expressions, each having its own distinctive interpretation of scripture and theological principles. Theologians who remained loyal to the pope saw this diversity within Christianity as chaotic, caused by the Protestants' rejection of the only thing capable of holding Christianity together, namely papal authority. Many Protestants, however, have looked upon the explosion of the new and diverse ways of practicing Christianity as a healthy development.

Whatever the case, Protestantism is known for its variety of expressions and ever-changing landscape, as new forms continue to emerge, older ones mutate, and others head into decline. A discussion of more recent forms of Protestantism is found in chapter six. This chapter focuses on five of its most established branches: Lutheranism, Calvinism, Anglicanism, Anabaptism, and Wesleyanism.

Lutheranism

Lutheranism takes its name from its founder Martin Luther. Despite his intense theological opposition to Roman Catholicism, Luther

This vision of the Last Supper, in which Jesus holds aloft the bread that represents his body, was created by Spanish artist Juan de Juanes in the sixteenth century.

revered its liturgy, or worship service. If one were to attend a Lutheran worship service today, one may well think that a Catholic Mass were taking place for the style of worship closely resembles that of a traditional Catholic service.

Lutherans, for example, believe in the real presence of Jesus in the Eucharist, the sacrament that re-enacts Jesus's giving of bread and wine to his disciples at the Last Supper before his crucifixion. They believe that Jesus mysteriously becomes present in a real, nonsymbolic way in the bread and the wine. (The Lutheran understanding of this "real presence" is slightly different from the Catholic view, a topic discussed in chapter four.) Perhaps the biggest difference with Catholic worship is the heightened emphasis Lutherans place on the sermon. Lutheran sermons often follow a format known as "Law and Gospel." In the sermons the inability of people to live up to the expectations of God as outlined in biblical law is juxtaposed with the forgiveness God extends to them in the person of Jesus. This forgiveness Lutherans celebrate as the heart of the gospel.

By the end of the sixteenth century, two thirds of Luther's home country, Germany, officially identified itself as Lutheran Christians. In 2004 approximately 25.8 million of Germany's Christians considered themselves Lutheran—31.3 percent of the population. In Scandinavia, Lutheranism became the official state religion in Denmark, Finland, Norway, and Sweden. With the exception of Sweden, which ended this arrangement in 2000, Lutheranism continues to enjoy varying degrees of official status in these countries. Scandinavian immigrants to the United States, who arrived as early as the seventeenth century and came in increasing numbers during the eighteenth and nineteenth centuries, brought their Lutheranism with them to North America. As most of these immigrants settled in the upper Midwest, that region of the United States continues to have the highest concentration of practicing Lutherans in North America. In 1988 three associations of American Lutherans—the American Lutheran Church, the Lutheran Church in America, and the American Evangelical Lutheran Church—united to form the Evangelical Lutheran Church in America (ELCA). This church today counts approximately five million people among its members. A more conservative and traditional group of American Lutherans, the Lutheran Church Missouri Synod (LCMS), did not join the ELCA. Its roughly 2.5 million members and 6,000 churches maintain their own identity separate from the ELCA.

In the tradition of its founder, the Lutheran tradition has produced an impressive number of renowned biblical scholars and theologians, many of whom have made significant contributions in their respective fields. Dietrich Bonhoeffer (1906–1945), for instance, one of the twentieth century's most respected Christian theologians, was a Lutheran who wrote some of the century's most profound theological books and essays. Bonhoeffer is also regarded by many as a modern-day martyr because he was executed in a concentration camp in Flossenbürg by the Nazis for his involvement, as a member of the German resistance, in a plot to assassinate Adolf Hitler.

Today, in a trend that mirrors all of Christianity in general, Lutheran membership in northern and western Europe is declining, but is growing rapidly in Asia, Latin America, and, especially, in Africa, the region that some people believe will become the center of Lutheranism in the twenty-first century.

calvinism

The Protestant movement known as Calvinism was named after its founder, John Calvin. He founded the first Calvinist community in 1541 in Geneva, Switzerland. He had fled his native France in 1534 during the persecution of French Protestants by the Catholic French monarch, Francis I. The other, earlier contributor to the tradition, Huldrych Zwingli (1484–1531) of Zurich, was instrumental in spreading the Protestant Reformation throughout Switzerland in advance of Calvin.

The defining documents of Calvinist orthodoxy are the Canons of the Synod of Dort (1618), which rejected the Arminian view of salvation, and the Westminster Confession of Faith (1647), which asserted that the Bible was the only infallible authority for the Christian faith and that there was a distinction to be made between the visible and the invisible church. Calvinist theology can be summarized by what are called its "Five Points," which one can remember using the mnemonic T-U-L-I-P: **T**otal depravity (the complete sinfulness of the human being, prior to salvation in Jesus), **U**nconditional divine election (human beings can do nothing on their own to be saved but must be elected to salvation by God), **L**imitation of the atonement to the elect (Jesus died on the cross only for those elected to salvation), **I**rresistibility of divine grace (no one can refuse God's election), and **P**erseverance in grace to the end (that is, once someone has been elected by God, that election is final and will not be revoked).

Unlike Lutheranism, Calvinist worship does not maintain the same degree of continuity with traditional Roman Catholic worship and liturgy. For instance, Calvinism rejects the notion of the "real presence" of Jesus Christ in the Eucharist. Zwingli maintained that the bread and wine were symbols of the crucified Jesus's body and blood and should not be understood as being transformed into the actual things themselves. Calvin, like Zwingli, was dissatisfied with the Lutheran and Roman Catholic understandings of real presence but chose to develop a new understanding of real presence, which will be discussed in chapter four.

Although Calvinism originated in both France and Switzerland, it took root especially in the Low Countries (Belgium, Luxemburg, the Netherlands) and Scotland. Its effect on the religious climate of the American colonies and then the United States was especially profound. At the time of the American Revolution in 1776, it was estimated that three fourths of the colonists had been somehow shaped by the Calvinist tradition. Eighteenth-century immigrants to America from the Low Countries further served to reinforce Calvinism as a major force on the American religious landscape.

Today, Calvinism lives on in American religious life mainly through the Presbyterian and Reformed churches, which have themselves split into factions due to disagreements over, among other things, how closely modern persons should follow John Calvin's theological prescriptions and how literally scripture should be interpreted. At the beginning of the twenty-first century, Calvinism is experiencing a rebirth in South Korea, South America, and Africa. In fact, the continents of Asia and Africa have the highest numbers of Christians represented in the World Alliance of Reformed Churches (WARC), a global organization of churches with Calvinist roots.

Calvinist theology enjoyed a revival in the twentieth century under the leadership of Karl Barth (1886–1968), a prolific Swiss theologian. Barth was active in the movement to rally German Christians against Adolf Hitler's National German Church, which blended Christianity with Nazi ideology. He also challenged Calvin's doctrine of double predestination and proposed instead that the logic of the Christian gospel pointed to a single predestination, or what is known in Christian theology as "universalism"—the teaching that all of humanity is elected by God to be saved in the person of Jesus; an election, in other words, from which no one is excluded.

Anglicanism

Anglicans trace their theological heritage to the Church of England, the existence of which, historians have discovered, dates to the first or second century C.E., when Christianity arrived in England. During the Middle Ages, the Church of England existed under the authority of the pope but split from the Roman Catholic Church in 1534, when King Henry VIII, frustrated by the pope's refusal to grant him a divorce, decreed that the British monarchy would run the Church in England. Today, the British monarchy serves as the head of the Church of England in a symbolic sense, while the actual duties of leadership fall to the archbishop of Canterbury, the spiritual leader of the worldwide Anglican Communion.

Anglicanism looks to one person, the archbishop of Canterbury, for guidance and spiritual leadership and is heavily invested in a hierarchical church structure in which bishops have significant power and authority over local congregations. Other Protestant denominations place more authority in the local congregations, thinking that a "top-down" model too closely resembles the Roman Catholic system of governance. Perhaps because of these differences, both the staunchest Protestants and Roman Catholics have looked on Anglicanism as embodying a middle way between their respective traditions. As a consequence of its position, Anglicanism has been active in the ecumenical movement, which attempts to reconcile the different branches of Christianity to create one, unified church.

Anglicanism's mediating position between Protestantism and Catholicism has not always been an easy one. At times in Anglican history, various persons and forces have tried to offset this balance and pull it in one direction or the other. Some of Anglicanism's central tenets, for instance, include such Protestant staples as justification by faith alone, participation by laypersons in church governance, and marriage for the clergy. Because its break from Rome was caused more by bureaucratic disputes than theological ones, Anglicanism has never been forced to outline its own distinct set of theological principles. It has, instead, relied on other Reformation traditions for its theological substance. During the latter half of the sixteenth century and the first quarter of the seventeenth (the time of the reigns of the British monarchs Elizabeth I and James I), Calvinism provided Anglicanism with its basic theological outlook. During the next 150 years, Lutheranism became Anglicanism's main theological influence. It is back to these Reformation roots that the more Protestant-oriented Anglicans have sought to bring Anglicanism.

A movement within Anglicanism known as Anglo-Catholicism stresses the more Catholic aspects of the Anglican tradition. Anglo-Catholics challenge the notion that their tradition began when Henry VIII wanted a divorce and claim that the Church of England dates to the first and second centuries C.E. through an unbroken succession of bishops in whose line the archbishop of Canterbury stands. For this reason, they look at Henry VIII's break from Rome as the restoration of the Church of England, not its creation. During the second half of the nineteenth century, Anglo-Catholics re-established religious orders and monastic communities within Anglicanism and during the twentieth century were at the forefront of Anglican-Roman Catholic ecumenical dialogues, conducted in the hope of fostering a greater spirit of unity and cooperation between the two churches.

Anglican worship closely resembles that of Roman Catholicism and shares with it a reverence for the Eucharist. The Anglican tradition of a uniform, common order of worship throughout all of its churches was initiated by Thomas Cranmer (1489–1556), an archbishop of Canterbury who compiled the Book of Common Prayer, Anglicanism's definitive guide to prayer and worship. Another important figure in Anglicanism was Richard Hooker (1554–1600), a parish priest who wrote the *Laws of Ecclesiastical Polity*, a significant work in Anglican theology.

In the United States, the Anglican tradition is represented by the Episcopal Church, which counted about 2.3 million persons as members in 2002. The Church became the center of controversy in the worldwide Anglican Communion when on June 7, 2003, its New Hampshire diocese elected V. Gene Robinson, an openly gay man, as bishop. Robinson, on November 2, 2003, became the world's first officially acknowledged gay Anglican bishop—an event that was met by the protests of some Anglicans who contend that homosexuality is a sin. As of 2006 Robinson continued to serve as the bishop of the diocese of New Hampshire, and Anglicanism was still experiencing the aftershocks of his historic appointment. Some people speculated that the Episcopal Church in the United States, if not the worldwide Anglican Communion itself, would split because of this issue.

Anabaptism

Historians associate the Protestant movement known as Anabaptism with the Radical Reformation. Anabaptism was unique in that it drew the scorn of Luther, Calvin, and the papal loyalists. Luther and Calvin both saw Anabaptism as a threat to the long-term survival of Protestantism because the kind of reformation the Anabaptists envisioned was significantly more radical and far reaching than anything either of them had in mind. The Anabaptists' refusal to accept any authority other than Jesus often placed them at odds with governing authorities. As a result, rulers cast a suspicious eye on Anabaptism, perceiving it to be a threat to the political and social stability of the regions under them.

Part of what made the Anabaptists in the sixteenth century unique and controversial was their rejection of the practice of infant baptism. They believed that only those individuals who were able to understand and to make a personal profession of faith should receive that sacrament. They called this believer's baptism. They thought that believer's baptism would encourage a more intentional and devout approach to the Christian life, as that rite of initiation into the church would then be the result of an individual's conscious choice, instead of the choice of one's parents. Anabaptists complained that Luther and Calvin's acceptance of infant baptism was keeping the Reformation from making a significant impact on the lives of Christians and that believer's baptism was the key to the transformation and renewal of the Christian faith in Europe. The name *Anabaptist* literally means "rebaptizer," which is fitting, as the Anabaptists, believing infant baptism to be invalid, taught that those adults who had been baptized as infants should be baptized again, following a public profession of their faith in Jesus.

There were four important expressions of or events related to Anabaptism in Europe at the time of the Reformation. The first was Thomas Müntzer's Peasants' War of 1524 to 1525 in Germany, which sought to take Luther's teachings regarding the equality of all persons before the authority of the Bible into the social and political realm through a violent revolt against the German nobility. The second expression was the Swiss Brethren, a group that brought the believer's baptism to Switzerland in 1525, practiced absolute pacifism, and taught that Christians should not participate in government. The third, led by Jacob Hutter, established communities in Moravia in which all property was owned and shared in common by the members. They became known as the Hutterites or the Hutterian Brethren. A fourth group of Anabaptists, known as the Mennonites after its founder Menno Simons (1496–1561), emphasized pacifist principles.

The largest contemporary group of Christians that traces its roots to the Anabaptists is the Baptists. John Smyth (1554–1612), an Englishman who relocated his persecuted church (on account of its endorsement of believer's baptism) to Amsterdam in 1608, is regarded as the founder of the Baptist movement.

Historically, Baptists have been divided between those who are largely Calvinist in their theological orientation and those who are more Arminian. Smyth's movement adopted Arminian principles and became known as General Baptists. Other Baptists located in London who were more Calvinist became known as Particular Baptists. These designations lasted throughout the sixteenth century.

In the seventeenth century, Baptists experienced a significant degree of persecution from the English crown until 1689, the year the Toleration Act was passed. This act decreed that nonconformists, that is, English Christians who were not loyal members of the Church of England, were free to worship in the churches of their own choosing but were barred from holding public office. Although they were viewed somewhat suspiciously in Europe, Baptists found a greater degree of acceptance in the American colonies. As early as 1636, the first Baptist church in America was founded in Providence, Rhode Island, by Roger Williams.

At the beginning of the twentieth century, Baptists in the United States were divided between the Southern Baptist Convention, established in 1845, and the Northern Baptist Convention (now known as the American Baptist Churches USA), founded in 1907.

In addition, a group of largely African American Northern Baptists split off from the Northern Baptist Convention in 1895 to form the National Baptist Convention, which itself eventually split off into two separate associations in 1915.

An important issue that Baptists faced in the twentieth century involved an ideological battle over the proper way to interpret the Bible. The modernists, who were open to contemporary scientific theories about creation and evolution, were pitted against the fundamentalists who rejected such theories in favor of literal readings of the creation accounts found in the book of Genesis. In these debates, the fundamentalist Baptists were led by southerner J. Frank Norris (1877–1952) and the modernists by Shailer Mathews (1863–1941) of Chicago.

Ideological battles and controversies over the proper way to read or interpret the Bible and the role of women in the Baptist churches continued throughout most of the twentieth century, resulting by 1984 in a proliferation of at least fifty-two different Baptist denominations in the United States. In 2005 the Southern Baptist Convention was the single largest organization of Baptists in the United States, with approximately 16.4 million members. It continues to be committed to a literal approach to biblical interpretation. Among the more famous American Baptists have been the evangelist Billy Graham (1918–) and civil rights leader Martin Luther King Jr. (1929–1968). Interestingly, unlike other Protestant denominations, whose membership demographics are dramatically shifting to the continents of South America, Africa, and Asia, it is projected that North America will retain 63 percent of the world's Baptists in 2010.

wesleyanism

Wesleyanism began as a reform movement within Anglicanism led by John Wesley (1703–1791), an Anglican priest. Like Luther, Wesley

A full house listens to the words of Billy Graham as he closes the 1964 American and Southern Baptist Conventions.

was a somewhat reluctant reformer, as he never imagined that the spiritual journey he was undertaking would cause a break within the Church of England. Oxford-educated, Wesley was truly one of the more remarkable figures in Christian history. In his lifetime, he preached more than 40,000 sermons and traveled close to 250,000 miles (402,336 kilometers)—on horseback—to deliver them.

The event that changed Wesley's life took place on May 24, 1738, when he felt, as he wrote in his journal, his heart "strangely warmed" while hearing Luther's preface to the letter to the Romans read aloud at a meeting he was attending. Before that experience, Wesley had struggled with the fact that for him the Christian faith was primarily an intellectual matter and not one that affected him in an experiential, heartfelt way. This bothered him, as he wanted to have what he could grasp with his mind be confirmed and received by his heart. In this experience Wesley felt that the connection between head and heart had at last been made. From that point on, Wesley, feeling as if this experience was indicative of a special call from God, pledged to devote his life to the cause of evangelism, or the public preaching of the Christian gospel in the hope of winning converts to the Christian faith.

Wesley met resistance from the Anglican establishment, which felt that his evangelistic activities were jeopardizing the Church of England's position as the center of English Christianity. The problem was that Wesley, when he was denied access to local Anglican pulpits, would preach sermons to people in open fields, town squares, hospitals, prisons, and schools. He was such an effective preacher and rhetorician that some of his audience would begin loudly weeping, publicly expressing regret over the sins they had committed, and sometimes collapse on the spot, overwhelmed by the emotional charge of Wesley's words. Wesley and the preachers who joined him in his cause began traveling throughout England, delivering their emotionally charged sermons wherever an audience was to be found. They became known as Methodists, which was initially a derogatory term. Eventually, they adopted the name as their own and turned it from a designation of derision to a badge of honor. The English lower and working classes, in particular, preferred Wesley's style of impassioned preaching to the staid and traditional Anglican liturgy, an indication that Wesley and the Methodists had exposed an inability in Anglicanism to connect the gospel message to everyday people on a personal, experiential, and emotional level. In addition, the Methodists revealed tendencies in Anglicanism toward styles of worship that were geared more to the liking of the noble and ruling classes. Traditional Anglicans feared that Wesley and his preachers, some of whom were not ordained clergy, would draw Anglican parishioners away from their local parishes.

Wesley and the Methodists eventually faced such firm resistance from Anglican authorities that they were forced to establish their own churches and clergy. This turn of events was much to Wesley's dismay, as he thought of Methodism as a renewal movement within Anglicanism, rather than something separate from it. Faced with the need to draft theological principles for the new Methodist church, Wesley combined Methodism's populist appeal with learned theology to create an expression of Protestant Christianity that remains viable to this day. Methodism's structure of authority became known as the Wesleyan Quadrilateral, as decisions and interpretations concerning Christian faith were adjudicated according to four criteria: scripture, tradition, reason, and experience.

Theologically, Wesley was committed to an Arminian form of Christianity and, by definition, rejected Calvinist notions of predestination and election. In addition, the Methodists developed a notion of "social holiness," an approach to Christianity that refused to compartmentalize the life of faith exclusively within the walls of the church. This motivated Methodists to be active and engaged

In many ways a grass-roots faith, rural convocations known as camp meetings were an important way Methodism was spread in the United States in the nineteenth century.

in English civil society. As it happened, the rise of Methodism in England coincided with the Industrial Revolution, which marked the transition from an economy based on agriculture to one based on factories and their products. In the midst of this upheaval, which disproportionately affected the laboring classes in the form of hazardous working conditions and decreased income, Methodism provided some stability, a sense of purpose, and a moral direction for those struggling to come to grips with their place in this new economy.

Methodism's emphasis on thrift, self-reliance, moral discipline (especially regarding alcohol consumption), and education helped to sustain the family structure of the English working classes at a time when economic forces were threatening to pull it apart.

Wesley and his movement also played a significant role in shaping the American religious landscape. Just as English Methodism appealed to the working poor during the Industrial Revolution, American Methodism served and ministered to those who were struggling to establish new lives for themselves on the American frontier. A highly organized group of Methodist preachers known as circuit riders made long journeys on horseback, shuttling between various frontier towns and settlements to sustain the faith of and win new converts among those on the front lines of the United States' western expansion.

In subsequent generations, the major elements of Wesley's Christianity—emotionally charged religion, populism, social activism, and strict moralism—were emphasized differently by separate groups, each claiming the mantle of authentic Wesleyanism. Mainline Methodism, for example, represented today by the United Methodist Church, has applied Wesley's notion of social holiness in recent years to large-scale problems and issues such as militarism and poverty, while the more conservative Wesleyan Holiness Movement continues to apply it to issues such as temperance (abstention from alcohol) and personal morality and piety. The two differ on theological matters, as well, with the former being more liberal in its theological orientation and the latter more conservative, particularly on the issue of biblical interpretation.

Statistical research indicates that Methodism, like many of the other expressions of mainline Protestantism, is declining in membership in Europe and North America but is growing in Africa and Asia. United Methodism in the United States reached its zenith, when judged by membership, in 1969, when it counted 10.9 million among its members. In 2002 that number dipped to 8.25 million—a 24 percent decline. By way of contrast, over a period of twenty-five years, membership in the Korean Methodist Church has doubled, rising from 600,000 in 1970 to 1.27 million in 1995. In the Methodist Church Nigeria, the number of members rocketed from 160,000 in 1970 to 1.5 million in 1995.

four

PROTESTANT WORSHIP

Like most of the other elements of protestantism, protestant worship is heavily informed by the Reformation doctrine of justification by faith alone. The first reformers used this doctrine in the interest of placing a Protestant theology of worship in contrast to the theology behind the Roman Catholic Mass. The Mass, for the first Protestants, was the embodiment of the "works-righteousness" approach to the Christian faith against which they were fighting. In their minds, Roman Catholics viewed the Mass as a kind of sacrifice the priest conducted so that they could experience God's grace. In contrast, the reformers saw Protestant worship as an act of thanksgiving for the grace that had already been freely given to the persons assembled. They held that Protestants should gather to worship God not so that the gifts of faith and grace might be received but in gratitude that God had granted these gifts to them in the first place.

Later ecumenical discussions revealed that the early reformers perhaps operated from too simplistic an understanding of the theology behind the Roman Catholic Mass and had, as a result, mischaracterized it. The doctrine of justification alone, nonetheless, continues to form the theoretical basis for most contemporary understandings of what Protestant worship is about, namely, a free response of praise and thanksgiving to God for what God has done and is doing for the world in the person of Jesus Christ.

With this in mind, we now turn to the specific content and defining features of Protestant worship, culminating in a discussion of Protestant preaching, an aspect of Christian worship for which Protestantism is, perhaps, best known.

worship: who, where, and when

The first and second of the Ten Commandments—"You shall have no other gods before me" and "You shall not make for yourself an idol . . . You shall not bow down to them or worship them" (Exodus 20:3–5)—serve as the guidelines that determine who is to be worshipped in Protestant communities of faith. In contrast to Roman Catholic worship, Protestants do not customarily invoke either angels or saints (human beings thought to stand as exemplars of the Christian faith) in the context of their worship services or in personal prayer. They have traditionally considered such activity to be violations of these commandments. In Protestant theology, only the Triune God—the Father, Son, and Holy Spirit—is to be worshipped or prayed to. Roman Catholics have often explained that angels and saints are prayed to or invoked not as ends in themselves but as intercessors or mediators between the faithful and the Triune God. The theological debate over this kind of intercessory prayer, a long-standing source of tension between Catholics and Protestants, continues at present, particularly with the renewed emphasis given to the Virgin Mary in Roman Catholic theology by Pope John Paul II (1920–2005). A number of Protestants feel that veneration of Mary, the mother of Jesus, comes close to violating the spirit of the first and second commandments.

There were no particulars established by the early reformers as to where Protestant worship was to occur. The first Protestants simply used existing meeting places, such as private buildings and their own homes, as houses of worship. As various forms of Protestantism grew older and more established, more "churchlike" buildings were constructed for the purpose of worship. Today, new forms of Protestantism, such as various Pentecostal movements, often meet for worship in homes, storefronts, and ordinary commercial buildings, just as the early Lutherans, Presbyterians, and Methodists once did.

Protestant worship space itself is arranged in a variety of ways, each according to the needs and dictates of the various denominations. In contrast to Roman Catholic or Eastern Orthodox churches, Protestant church buildings are, with Anglican churches and cathedrals as the exception, customarily less ornate, with minimalist altars that often consist of a bare cross (rather than a crucifix, a cross on which the figure of Jesus is placed), a few candles, and perhaps some stained glass in the windows. The theological rationale for this is rooted in the second commandment's prohibition against the adoration of idols and the belief that excessive ornamentation distracts the worshipper from focusing on the reading and hearing of scripture and the minister's sermon. As the reading of scripture and preaching are at the heart of Protestant worship, lecterns for the former and pulpits for the latter are important components of the design of Protestant worship space.

The time of worship, for most Protestants, falls on Sunday morning, the day, according to Christian tradition, on which Jesus rose from the dead. It is for this reason that the Sabbath, in accordance with the fourth commandment (Exodus 20:8–11), is commonly observed on this particular day of the week. A small percentage of Protestants, most notably the Seventh-day Adventists, observe the Sabbath on Saturday and hold their worship services on that day. Some Protestants, including the English Puritans and some Scottish Calvinists in the seventeenth century, were active in the movement known as Sabbatarianism, which strove to devote the Sabbath exclusively to prayer, worship, and general religious observance. Sabbatarianism in the United States led to the passage of "blue laws," which mandate the closing of certain businesses on Sundays. Blue laws still exist in certain communities but are not as common as they were at one time when Protestantism was a more prevalent cultural force.

sacraments: Baptism and the Lord's Supper

In the world of Christian theology, sacraments have been defined as "visible signs of an inward grace," that is, as concrete representations of a reality that is not detectable by the five physical senses. They are understood by Christians as seals of God's promises, tangible ways that God's grace—God's steadfast love for creation—can be grasped. For this reason, they are very important in Christian worship.

In the Roman Catholic tradition, there are seven sacraments: baptism, confirmation, the Eucharist (communion), penance (confession), anointing of the sick or dying, holy orders (ordination to religious life), and holy matrimony. Most Protestants recognize only two sacraments: baptism and the Eucharist, or what many Protestants refer to as the "Lord's Supper." Protestants believe that the only legitimate sacraments are those that the New Testament records Jesus as having directly instituted for the whole Church. From the perspective of most Protestants, only baptism and the Lord's Supper fall into that category.

Baptism is the rite that marks the beginning of the individual's life of faith through the visible sign of water. Baptism signifies the re-establishment of right relationships between God and God's creation through the overcoming of original sin. The central debate regarding this sacrament within Protestantism concerns the appropriate time at which baptism should be received. Protestant denominations whose heritages are located in either the Calvinist, Lutheran, or Anglican traditions find the practice of infant baptism acceptable. Those rooted in Anabaptist traditions reject that practice in favor of a "believer's baptism" in which only those individuals capable of making a

Baptism is a key Protestant sacrament and rite. This woman is immersed in water at a mass baptism ceremony in Newport News, Virginia, in September 1939.

responsible, public profession of faith are to be baptized. The ritual itself is also practiced differently according to the denomination. Some sprinkle or lightly pour water over the head of the individual. Others seeking to represent more exactly Jesus's own baptism in the river Jordan (Matthew 3:13–17, Mark 1:9–11, Luke 3:21–22, John 1:31–34), fully immerse or lower individuals below the surface of the water and lift them out again—a more dramatic symbol of their transition from "death" in original sin to "life" in Jesus.

Disagreements among Protestants have also occurred over the proper understanding of the sacrament of the Lord's Supper, the visible sign that signifies, through bread and wine, the sacrifice that Christians believe Jesus made on humanity's behalf through his death on the cross. Specifically, Protestants have debated whether the body and blood of Jesus are actually present in the Eucharistic bread and wine. Swiss reformer Huldrych Zwingli contended that the Lord's Supper should be understood only as a remembrance of Jesus's broken body and blood shed on the cross, in accordance with Jesus's command to "Do this in remembrance of me." (Luke 22:19)

Luther sought an understanding that avoided seeing the Lord's Supper as a mere commemorative act and made room for the presence of Jesus in the bread and the wine. In this respect, Luther echoed the Roman Catholic tradition and emphasized Jesus's declaration "This is my body" (Matthew 26:26, Mark 14:22, and Luke 22:19). Luther differentiated his view by arguing that Jesus was present in the bread and the wine not because of the priest's words or actions, but because of Jesus's promise to be there and because Jesus, as the second person of the Trinity, was already present everywhere. Calvin argued for yet a third understanding. His belief was that Jesus is present in the Lord's Supper, not by his indwelling in the elements of bread and wine, but through the power of the Holy Spirit to raise the person who partakes of the bread and the wine into the heavenly presence of the crucified, risen, and ascended Jesus.

From a modern perspective, such discussions of the ways in which Jesus is present in the Lord's Supper may seem either unimportant or too fantastical to be taken seriously. Partly for this reason, as the years that separate Protestants from Luther and Calvin have increased, and with Protestants becoming less likely to adopt theological positions that appear far-fetched from a rationalist perspective, for many worshippers notions of Jesus's real presence in the Lord's Supper have become less of a concern. Zwingli's view of the Lord's Supper as a ritual that functions simply as a memorial of Jesus's sacrifice on the cross has become the predominant view in many Protestant denominations. This trend began to reverse slightly in the wake of the ecumenical movement of the mid-twentieth century, a movement whose goal was to promote a spirit of unity among the three branches of Christianity—Roman Catholicism, Protestantism, and Eastern Orthodoxy. The leaders of the ecumenical movement argued that the sacraments, especially the Lord's Supper, should have a greater emphasis in Protestant worship. Among some Protestant denominations, this led to a renewed examination of Luther and Calvin's understandings of how Jesus is present to the believer in the sacrament of the Lord's Supper.

MUSIC

One of the most significant innovations the early reformers made stemmed from their belief that Christian worship should be conducted in the native language of the people. The Roman Catholic Church traditionally insisted upon the use of Latin in worship until the reforms of the Second Vatican Council (1962–1965). Protestants turning away from Latin led to the writing of devotional songs and hymns in French, German, and English, among other languages, to be sung in worship services. As a result, music has played an important role in Protestant worship and, reciprocally, Protestantism has played a significant role in the history of Western music.

Because Luther was a great music enthusiast and wanted it to have an important role in Lutheran worship, Lutherans wrote most of the early Protestant hymns. Calvin, in contrast, limited the songs to be sung in worship to the Psalms of the Bible and deemed new compositions inappropriate for worship. Later, the English began writing some of Christianity's most famous hymns. Notable among them are those by Charles Wesley (1707–1788), the brother of Methodism's founder John Wesley. In the Baroque era, which extended from the early 1600s through the mid-1700s, European Protestant music reached a high point with Johann Sebastian Bach's cantatas and Passions and George Frederick Handel's oratorios, the most renowned of which is his *Messiah*.

In subsequent centuries, certain Protestant communities continued to adhere to Calvin's restriction of music to the singing of Psalms. Most Protestants, however, encouraged the writing and use of hymns that combined devotional lyrics with melodies that were both culturally resonant and popular. Among North American Protestant communities, new hymns written to the melodies of American folk songs became popular and were interspersed among the older, European hymns in worship services. These uniquely American hymns and spirituals eventually led to the rise of gospel music, particularly in African American Protestant churches. Gospel music is regarded today as an original American art form. Many renowned African American musicians, songwriters, and performers began their careers in church, including Thomas Dorsey (1899–1993), known as the "father of gospel music." Some of the pioneers of American rock 'n' roll—Little Richard, Elvis Presley, Jerry Lee Lewis, and Sam Cooke—

created their sound by drawing on American gospel music. Today, many Protestant worship services include contemporary-sounding music. Some churches, especially nondenominational evangelical churches, incorporate high energy, rocklike anthems into their services. Mainline Protestants, for the most part, have retained the more traditional hymns as their music of choice in worship.

protestant preaching

Protestant preaching, in the form of the sermon or a reflection on a biblical passage addressed to a congregation, resides at the center of most Protestant worship. This emphasis on the sermon can be traced to Romans 10:17, among other New Testament passages, in which Paul writes that "faith comes from what is heard, and what is heard comes through the word of Christ." Hearing is made primary, and not seeing or believing, because the Christian message was first conceptualized by the early Christians as news—that is, as the person-to-person broadcast of the event that they believed transformed the world: the life, death, and resurrection of Jesus. The word *gospel* means "good news," signifying that, in its first-century context, the gospel was not considered to be so much a collection of moral teachings or sayings on which to meditate as it was an announcement of something that had happened—in the manner in which newspapers today announce the results of a presidential election, the end of a war, or a monumental scientific discovery. That this occurrence, the basis of the Christian faith, was conceived as a news event makes sense because the conviction that God had taken on human form, died the death of a common criminal, and rose from the dead three days later was something so outside the realm of everyday experience that one could only be told about it, not deduce it through reason or logic. Christian preaching is seen by Christians as the continuation of the reporting of this news.

Preaching and attesting to one's faith are seen as key elements in Protestant worship.

Luther was insistent that Christian preaching not only consist of the reporting of this news to the gathered community, but also include an account of its contemporary significance for the hearer.

> . . . it is not enough or in any sense Christian to preach the works, life, and words of Christ as historical facts, as if the knowledge of these would suffice for the conduct of life. . . . Rather ought Christ to be preached to the end that faith in him may be established that he may not only be Christ, but be Christ for you and me, and that what is said of him and is denoted in his name may be effectual in us. Such faith is produced and preserved in us by preaching why Christ came, what he brought and bestowed, what benefit it is to us to accept him.

As the passage above indicates, Luther believed that it was not enough for a preacher to simply tell the story of Jesus's life. One also had to discuss why this particular life was significant to the person listening. It was this latter component, Luther believed, that would plant the seed of faith in the heart of the hearer. In many Protestant denominations, people listening to the sermon are open to the possibility that God will work through the words of the minister to impart faith to their hearts and minds. This possibility is another reason why the sermon is often considered to be the heart of worship for Protestants.

preaching and revelation

There were differences of opinion among the early reformers as to the nature of the relationship between human preaching and revelation, or what Christians believe to be the act of God making God's self known to human beings through faith. Some felt that human proclamation of the good news about Jesus could itself be considered

God's own word. Swiss reformer Huldrych Zwingli, however, was wary of this equation and differentiated between what he called the "external word of God," or preaching, from "the internal word of God," which he believed occurred when the Holy Spirit worked within the human heart to reveal God to that person. Calvin adopted a position somewhere between these two. He determined that human preaching can become God's own word only when God, through the power of the Holy Spirit, elects human words to be revelatory.

Those who think the authority of the Word is dragged down by the baseness of the men called to teach it disclose their own ungratefulness. For, among the many excellent gifts with which God has adorned the human race, it is a singular privilege that he deigns to consecrate to himself the mouths and tongues of men in order that his voice may resound in them. . . . For, although God's power is not bound to ordinary means, he has nonetheless bound us to this ordinary manner of teaching. . . . In order, then, that pure simplicity of faith may flourish among us, let us not be reluctant to use this exercise of religion [preaching] which God, by ordaining it, has shown us to be necessary and highly approved.

Anabaptists found such elevated views of human preaching suspect as they failed to distinguish between God's words and actions and those of human beings. Anabaptist worship emphasized prayer and a more democratic approach to preaching in which anyone who felt moved by the Holy Spirit, laity and clergy alike, could address the congregation extemporaneously. Such addresses, for the Anabaptists, could never be equated with God's own word but were seen as simple human testimonials to the power and efficacy of faith in God.

The evolution of protestant preaching

Protestant preaching has undergone some notable transitions and continues to change and evolve. In both the early Lutheran and Calvinist traditions, sermons usually fell into one of two main categories: expository, in which a particular text from the Bible was the subject, or catechetical, in which one of Christianity's central doctrines or creeds was discussed. In the eighteenth and nineteenth centuries, with the rise of Pietism, a form of Protestantism that emphasized the experiential and emotional dimensions of the Christian faith, a third kind of preaching emerged. It made the listener's direct experience of faith and salvation the subject of the sermon. Thus, the believer's inner life, the personal benefits of faith, and the importance of "giving one's heart to Jesus" became the focus of this new type of sermon. In North America, this form of preaching became widespread.

Some historians believe that the dynamic English Methodist preacher George Whitefield, on his 1739 preaching tour of the American colonies, introduced this impassioned Pietist preaching style to American Protestant congregations. According to these interpretations, Whitefield was the spark that ignited the Great Awakening in North America, a time in the eighteenth century when there was an explosion of intense religiosity. The preaching of Northampton, Massachusetts, minister Jonathan Edwards (1703–1758) also served to sustain this groundswell of newfound American religiosity.

In the nineteenth century, the emotionally charged preaching style of Whitefield and Edwards was further developed by Charles G. Finney (1792–1875), who had begun to draw the connection in his sermons between the individual experience of faith and larger social issues such as slavery, whose abolition Finney called for, and temperance, or abstention from alcohol, which he championed. Heirs to Finney, such as Dwight L. Moody (1837–1899) and former professional baseball player Billy Sunday (1862–1935) added other components to Finney's style, such as calling on an audience to make personal commitments to Jesus (Moody) and incorporating entertainment and showmanship into preaching (Sunday).

Another notable branch of the American Protestant preaching tradition is the African American one, which took the Finney approach and added to it a unique, rhythmic style that continues in many African American churches. Researchers have looked into the connection between this African American preaching style and traditional African patterns in music and speech in which the call and response between preacher and congregation is thought to reflect certain indigenous African practices. Africans, brought to North America and enslaved, fused these two styles, it is argued, following the mass conversion of African slaves to Christianity during the American Great Awakening. This dynamic style was ingrained into the American consciousness by what is perhaps the most famous of all twentieth-century American sermons: Dr. Martin Luther King Jr.'s "I have a dream" speech. In this address, brilliantly delivered on August 28, 1963—the culmination of the historic March on Washington—King, a Baptist minister, creatively and effectively wove the biblical theme of liberation from bondage with an appeal to the deep-seated American principle of human equality before the law to speak to the plight of African Americans suffering under legalized segregation and oppression, particularly in the American South.

The Liberal-fundamentalist Divide and New Evangelicalism

A theological division began to emerge in American Protestantism at the turn of the twentieth century that further affected both the style and the content of Protestant preaching. This division was between "fundamentalists" who stressed the literal truth of the Bible on all matters and subjects, even when it conflicted with modern science, and "liberals" who rejected the biblical literalism of the fundamentalists and sought to harmonize the Christian faith with modern science and contemporary culture.

At the center of the liberal-fundamentalist storm was Harry Emerson Fosdick (1878–1969), a popular preacher who championed the cause of liberal Protestants against the fundamentalists, most notably in a sermon he delivered on May 21, 1922, from the pulpit of the First Presbyterian Church in New York City, entitled "Shall the Fundamentalists Win?" Following this sermon, Fosdick was forced out of the Presbyterian Church by a group of prominent, theologically conservative, and fundamentalist-leaning Presbyterians that included former presidential candidate William Jennings Bryan (1860–1925) and theologian John Gresham Machen (1881–1937). John D. Rockefeller Jr. (1874–1960), the wealthiest man in the United States at that time and an ardent supporter of Fosdick, came to his favorite preacher's rescue by constructing for Fosdick the magnificent Riverside Church in New York City. From the Riverside pulpit, which quickly became the mouthpiece of American liberal Protestantism, Fosdick preached more than 650 sermons and developed a unique style that became known as the "life-situation" or "problem-centered" sermon.

Fosdick discussed his new style in an essay he wrote for the July 1928 issue of *Harper's Magazine*, entitled "What Is the Matter with Preaching?" In that essay, Fosdick argued that the starting point of modern Protestant preaching should be the existential, or immediately personal, situation of the individual in the congregation. The preacher should then address the hearer's existential situation by combining biblical and theological insights with secular psychological, philosophical, and literary illustrations. Fosdick's critics from the Protestant theological right charged that in his sermons the scale was tipped in favor of secular sources, with the Bible and traditional Christian theology receiving too limited of a focus. Fosdick's supporters insisted that his was the only style capable of bringing modern and educated persons into the church. Whatever the case, Fosdick's preaching formula propelled Protestant liberalism to a prestigious position in American society during the middle of the twentieth century, with its ministers and theologians advising presidents, writing articles in widely circulated magazines, and delivering lectures to packed auditoriums in colleges and universities.

Over the past thirty years or so, the influence of liberal Protestantism on American society has lessened, which some people attribute to the Fosdick preaching style. The problem, some believe, was that after listening to preachers who drew heavily from secular disciplines, such as psychology, lay Protestant liberals decided to cut out the middle man— the liberal preacher. This may account, in part, for the rise in popularity and the increased business of professional psychologists and self-help experts in the latter half of the twentieth century. In addition, a number of the baby boom generation, those born between the years 1946 and 1964, grew suspicious of established centers of authority, such as the government, the military, and the church, during their involvement with the civil rights movement, the mass protests against the Vietnam War, and the feminist cause. Many rebelled against what they perceived as a "white male Protestant establishment" in the United States that was resistant to change.

Into this vacuum stepped a new kind of Protestantism, called new evangelicalism. Its sermons combined a reverence for biblical authority, which in some cases led to a full-fledged adoption of biblical fundamentalism, a charismatic and entertaining preaching style reminiscent of Billy Sunday, and aspects of the Fosdick style, such as the focus on the personal and situational. The social appeal and potential political power of new evangelicalism became apparent as early as 1949, the year evangelist Billy Graham preached in Los Angeles before the first of his consistently well-attended "crusades," or mass revivals that were orchestrated to encourage the making of "personal commitments" to Jesus. It was not unusual in subsequent years for Graham to preach before audiences numbering more than 100,000 persons.

With the spread of mass media in American culture, certain Protestant evangelicals who patterned themselves after Graham became adept at preaching before television cameras and cornered the market on what became known as televangelism. Protestant liberals largely avoided mass media, thinking it too hucksterish and opportunistic for their tastes. The liberals resolved to limit their preaching to local church pulpits. But huge evangelical "megachurches," fueled perhaps by the televangelist movement, began to dwarf, in terms of membership, the established mainline Protestant churches, such as the United Methodist, Lutheran, and Episcopal churches. The high-energy worship services of the megachurches—which offered contemporary, inspirational music and dramatic sermons that combined self-help philosophy, biblical instruction, and moral direction—proved to be a highly successful formula for attracting new members toward the end of the twentieth century.

Some people question whether the preaching of the new Protestant evangelicalism is falling into the same pattern as the old liberal style of Fosdick by drifting too much into the realm of pop-psychology, with sermons centered more on the promotion of self-esteem and self-empowerment than on biblical theology. Similar questions

A parishioner emotionally professes his faith during a 2005 Sunday service in South Barrington, Illinois. The megachurch these followers belong to draws an average of 20,000 worshippers to each service.

are being asked of new evangelical movements whose preachers foster a consumerist mentality through the preaching of "prosperity gospels" that teach that there is a direct correlation between one's degree of faith and one's ability to accumulate wealth. If such trends continue, the future may see a backlash against such preaching with a movement that emphasizes more traditional Christian themes such as God's condemnation and judgment of human pride, wealth, and materialism.

five

SOCIETY, CULTURE, AND POLITICS

one of the defining historical characteristics of protestantism has been its refusal to stay confined to a given sphere, be it the walls of its churches, the oceans that demarcate its native continents, or opinions about what its place should be in the political arena. From its inception, the theological positions it championed had wide-ranging societal, cultural, and political ramifications that transformed Europe. Sometimes, the results were tragic. The Thirty Years' War (1618–1648), for instance, which claimed many lives and decimated villages, towns, and cities throughout Europe, was caused in large part by the enmity that resulted from Protestant-Catholic divisions. More recently, in Northern Ireland, Protestant unionists, who want Northern Ireland to remain a part of the United Kingdom, and Catholic nationalists, who want Northern Ireland to become independent, have spilled one another's blood in the fight to determine the region's future. In each case, militant factions have justified their warmongering by appealing to one side or another of the Christian theological divide that the Reformation introduced.

In other instances, Protestantism has been a progressive, life-affirming force in the societies and cultures it has reached. Its belief in the importance of individuals encountering the Bible for themselves and in their own language was instrumental in raising the level of education among the general European population. Protestantism, in addition, has been the driving force behind a number of political and social movements that sought the construction of economic safety nets and systemic support for the most vulnerable members of human society.

Three particular times, places, and cultures—Puritanism, the social gospel movement, and African American Protestantism—highlight the tremendous impact Protestantism has had on the Western world and the wide-ranging ways its influence has been acutley felt.

puritanism

Puritanism was a movement within Protestantism that began in England during the reign of Elizabeth I (1558–1603). It would later arrive in North America where, during the English colonial period, Puritanism reached its high point in terms of societal power and cultural influence.

Initially the term *puritan* carried negative connotations and referred to someone whose approach to Christianity was exclusively moralistic. In the sixteenth and seventeenth centuries, the word was specifically used to identify persons who were critical of the Church of England for what they saw as its general lack of religiosity and moral standards. Part of the reason why these Puritans were so focused on the degree of one's religiosity and moral uprightness was because Puritanism's theological emphasis was on the kind of life one should live after receiving justification by faith alone. By focusing on this aspect, the Puritans brought to light two different understandings of the human being in light of the gospel of Jesus. These views were rooted in the original theologies of Luther and Calvin.

Luther summarized his theology in the Latin phrase *simul iustus et simul peccator*, which means "at the same time both righteous and a sinner." For Luther, the individual, before receiving the grace of

God through Jesus, was *totaliter peccator*—a total sinner—as there was nothing one could do, in and of one's self, to become righteous in God's sight. The human being, after receiving justification, became at once completely righteous, because, on account of Jesus's death and resurrection, God no longer counted people's sinfulness against them. At the same time, individuals were viewed as total sinners because this righteousness belonged not to the person but to Jesus. Consequently, Luther asserted that justified human beings possessed no innate righteousness of which they could boast. As such, the righteousness of the Christian came from an external source, which was why Luther called it a "passive" or "alien" righteousness:

> **These two things are quite contrary: to wit, that a Christian is righteous and beloved of God, and yet notwithstanding he is a sinner. For God cannot deny his own nature: that is, he must needs hate sin and sinners; and this he doth of necessity, for otherwise he should be unrighteous and love sin. How then can these two contradictories stand together: I am a sinner, and most worthy of God's wrath and indignation; and yet the Father loveth me? Here nothing cometh between, but only Christ the mediator. The Father, saith he [Christ], doth not therefore love you because ye are worthy of love, but because ye have loved me, and have believed that I came out from him. . . . Therefore it is necessary that we should have imputation [i.e., the external granting] of righteousness, which we obtain through Christ and for Christ's sake, who is given unto us and received of us by faith.**

Calvin stressed, like Luther, that the justification of the human being was an unmerited gift from God but believed that those who had been elected by God would progress in such a way that their status as total sinners would lessen over time:

If we share in his resurrection, through it we are raised up into newness of life to correspond with the righteousness of God . . . . In this way it pleases the Lord fully to restore whomsoever he adopts into the inheritance of life. And indeed, this restoration does not take place in one moment or one day or one year; but through continual and sometimes even slow advances God wipes out in his elect the corruptions of the flesh, cleanses them of guilt, consecrates them to himself as temples renewing all their minds to true purity that they may practice repentance throughout their lives and know that this warfare will end only at death.

What Calvin described captures the objective of the Puritan movement, namely, the promotion of the moral purification of the Christian person by the inner workings of the Holy Spirit. The Puritans also held, like Calvin, that only the elect would be given the ability to move toward moral purity. They deduced that it was possible to identify who was among the elect by carefully observing a person's degree of moral uprightness. What developed among the Puritans was a perpetual anxiety about whether they could truly count themselves among God's elect—an anxiety that they attempted to ease by being as morally rigorous as possible, as their degree of success in that regard would indicate, according to their logic, whether they were among God's chosen. However, who was and was not among the elect was something that could only be known to God, Calvin argued, and he warned human beings against trying to determine such things from their limited, finite perspectives.

Despite Calvin's warnings, determining these things was what the Puritans aimed to do and what made their approach to Christianity so controversial. They attempted to identify those people in their church communities whose moral purity earmarked them as among the elect. By distinguishing those individuals from other church members whose conduct, they judged, indicated that they were not among God's chosen, the Puritans believed it possible to create a purified church composed only of God's elect. This practice was judged by the authorities in the Church of England to be disruptive, and, in part, led to the state-sponsored persecution that drove the Puritans to establish new lives for themselves in the British-controlled American colonies. A significant number arrived on the *Mayflower* in 1620.

In North America, the Puritans worked hard to construct the kind of well-regulated, morally disciplined Christian society that had eluded them. They came to

view their trip across the Atlantic Ocean as part of God's plan for them to create the kind of purified Christianity that had failed to materialize in Europe. The colony of Plymouth in New England would become the site of the Puritans' most ambitious social experiment. There they hoped to establish a Christian community that would serve as an example to the rest of the world.

Before long some clergy and noted laypersons in the colonies spoke out against certain Puritan practices. Among them were Boston minister

Dressed in plain garments, a group of Puritans makes its way through the snow to a Sunday worship service. Their strict code of conduct informed the early social life of the United States in the colonial era, particularly in their home base of New England.

John Cotton and Anne Hutchinson. They accused the movement of abandoning the doctrine of justification by faith alone in favor of "works righteousness" or a merit-based approach to salvation in Jesus. Puritan leaders, for their part, charged Cotton and Hutchinson with promoting antinomianism, or a theologically justified disregard for moral and ethical standards, which, interestingly, Luther's Roman Catholic opponents also accused him of in the sixteenth century.

From the perspective of the Puritans, dissent was a sign not of a vibrant, freethinking community but of impending social chaos. It was an attack on their efforts to construct the purified form of Christianity toward which they believed God's providence was leading them. Truth, they firmly believed, was readily apparent to those who earnestly sought it through the Bible. Consensus was a clear sign that the community's actions reflected God's will, and dissension an indication that resistance to it was afoot. Disciplinary actions such as whippings, the levying of fines, and incarceration were exacted in an effort to curb dissent. In a few extreme cases, executions were carried out. Eventually, the English king William III stepped in and demanded that statutes be put in place to curb Puritan zeal and allow for a measure of religious tolerance within the colony of Massachusetts.

Today, Puritanism no longer exists in the explicit form of an actual Protestant denomination, although as long as there are religious communities, the spirit of Puritanism—the impulse to distinguish dedicated, true believers from those thought to be less so—will undoubtedly endure. The formal church structure established by the Puritans, however, continues in Congregationalism, a form of Protestantism that locates the center of all religious authority in the local community itself, not in a bishop or a superintendent. (The United Church of Christ is one contemporary Protestant denomination that follows this form of church governance.) Later generations of American Puritans joined Presbyterian churches, as their common Calvinist heritage often made them compatible. Other Congregationalist churches abandoned the Protestant Christian fold altogether by embracing Unitarianism, a religion that, while loosely based on Christian principles, rejected the doctrine of the Trinity in favor of a monotheism that they found more rational.

Though largely derided in noted American literary works such as Nathaniel Hawthorne's novel *The Scarlet Letter* (1850) and Arthur Miller's play *The Crucible* (1953), Puritanism has long been a source of interest for American historians, psychologists, and sociologists. German sociologist Max Weber contended that Puritanism was essential to the development and rise of market capitalism in the Western world. Weber's thesis, elaborated in his book *The Protestant Ethic and the Spirit of Capitalism* (1904–1905), is that Protestantism in general, but Puritanism specifically, established the societal and cultural foundation for capitalism, primarily through the Puritans' belief that personal success was a sign that one was among God's elect. This belief justified in the Puritan mind the desire to seek profits in business, which, when coupled with the Calvinist and Puritan emphasis on thrift, hard work, self-discipline, and personal responsibility, created a philosophy of life that was a perfect fit for a society built around market capitalism. Taking the United States as an example, a nation in whose early life Puritanism played a key role and that would become the most successful capitalist nation in the world, some readers found Weber's thesis to have been not only strengthened but also historically vindicated.

The social gospel

In the late nineteenth and early twentieth century, a Protestant social movement known as the social gospel sought to take the gospel of Jesus beyond the confines of church walls and into the world where, it was hoped, it would transform society as well as individuals. This movement differed from Puritanism in a number of key aspects. First, the social gospel did not proceed from the assumption that societal transformation began with the inner life of the individual. Rather, its leaders believed that the proper starting point was the reformation of the larger systems and structures that governed society. In this respect, the social gospel movement reflected the prevailing spirit of the political and economic times in the United States during the period from the 1890s to the 1920s referred to as the Progressive Era. During this time, many Americans pushed for structural changes and governmental intervention that they thought would reduce the general poverty rate, raise standards of living among the lower classes, and regulate the big businesses that, prior to the rise of the labor movement, were neither obligated nor pressured to extend benefits or minimum wages to their workers. The social gospel reflected the contribution of mainline American Protestantism to this effort to solve many of the problems resulting from the newly industrialized American economy.

The ideology that the social gospel sought to counter was social Darwinism, which attempted to apply Darwin's theory of natural selection to explain why certain individuals in society were wealthier and more successful than others. Social Darwinists believed that poverty was not caused by injustice, oppression, or a big business's failure to pay its workers a decent wage. Rather, it was a sign of an individual's inability to adapt to his or her economic environment and indicated the innate inferiority of the poor in comparison to the wealthy. Critics of social Darwinism charged that the theory failed to account for the concentration of wealth in certain families that simply passed it down from one generation to the next and the many talented persons whose economic class kept them from the opportunities readily available to the wealthy and elite. The social gospel combined this criticism with an emphasis upon Jesus's particular concern for the plight of the poor and oppressed, as evidenced in these New Testament passages:

> **If you wish to be perfect, go, sell your possessions, and give money to the poor, and you will have treasure in heaven; then come, follow me. (Matthew 19:21)**

> **The Spirit of the Lord is upon me, because he has anointed me to bring good news to the poor. (Luke 4:18a)**

**Blessed are you who are poor, for yours is the kingdom of
God. Blessed are you who are hungry now, for you will be
filled. . . . But woe to you who are rich, for you have received
your consolation. Woe to you who are full now, for you will
be hungry. (Luke 20:20b–21, 24–25a)**

Such New Testament verses became the rallying cry for
the social gospel and led its participants toward a theological
reinterpretation of the essence of Christianity. Where Protestant
Christianity in the past emphasized the need to secure one's place
in heaven after death, the social gospel talked about the need
to work for the establishment of what Jesus referred to as the
Kingdom of God on earth—a kingdom in which justice, peace,
and equality would reign. Where Protestants were at one time
urged to let Jesus into their individual hearts, the social gospel
taught that they were to seek him in the faces of the poor they
were called to serve. (Matthew 25:31–46) In essence, the social
gospel called for a turn toward what is called in Christian theology
God's immanence, or God's indwelling presence in creation, and
less of an emphasis on God's transcendence, or God's distance and
difference from the created order. This shift in emphasis is evident
in the work of the social gospel's theological proponent, Walter
Rauschenbusch (1861–1918):

**The social gospel is the old message of salvation, but enlarged
and intensified. The individualistic gospel has taught us to
see the sinfulness of every human heart and has inspired us
with faith in the willingness and power of God to save every
soul that comes to him. But it has not given us an adequate
understanding of the sinfulness of the social order and its
share in the sins of all individuals within it. It has not evoked
faith in the will and power of God to redeem the permanent**

institutions of human society from their inherited guilt of oppression and extortion. Both our sense of sin and our faith in salvation have fallen short of the realities under its teaching. The social gospel seeks to bring men under repentance for their collective sins and to create a more sensitive and more modern conscience. It calls on us for the faith of the old prophets who believed in the salvation of nations.

On the front lines of the social gospel movement were Protestant women who, historically, had been largely relegated to the sidelines by Protestant men. Prominent among these activists was Jane Addams (1860–1935), whose settlement house movement offered support for recent immigrants to the United States and the poor. Another crusader for the social gospel was Frances Willard, leader of the Woman's Christian Temperance Union (WCTU), an organization that was instrumental in the passing of the Eighteenth Amendment in 1919, which banned the sale of alcohol in the United States (it was repealed in 1933). Willard and the WCTU believed that alcohol consumption was a leading cause of poverty as it often caused women and children to be neglected or abandoned altogether by drinking husbands who were usually their sole source of financial security.

While the social gospel's influence over American Protestantism waned by the middle of the twentieth century, it played a significant role in the American Progressive movement by generating the momentum that led to the federally sponsored economic programs, collectively known as the New Deal, that were drafted by President Franklin Roosevelt and passed by Congress to help alleviate the widespread poverty of the Great Depression of the 1930s. One social problem that the largely white social gospel movement failed to address was the legalized racial discrimination common in the United States during that time. African American Protestant Christians, with their churches as their base of operations, would have to fight and win this battle primarily on their own in the decades that followed.

Protestantism and its various sects helped trigger a period of social reform, particularly in the United States, in the late eighteenth and early nineteenth centuries. This 1874 Currier and Ives print shows the crusading women of the Temperance League smashing barrels of alcohol. The Eighteenth Amendment, which banned the sale of alcohol and ushered in the period known as Prohibition, soon followed in the late 1910s.

african american protestantism: The struggle for freedom

For Protestantism in general, African American Protestantism is a source of both shame and pride. Shame because white slaveholders used Protestant Christianity and the Bible to pacify African slaves in the American South and to justify their dehumanization at the hands of their white owners. Pride because both the abolitionist and civil rights movements stand today as one of the most moving, powerful, and positive examples of Christian faith in action that the world has, perhaps, ever seen.

African slaves were first brought to North America by Dutch traders and sold to colonists in Jamestown, Virginia, in 1619. Documents show that the earliest recorded baptism of a slave occurred in Massachusetts in 1641, but most Africans in North America practiced traditional African religions that were completely unrelated to Christianity. In the mid-1700s, at the time of the Great Awakening, the African American population began to embrace Protestant Christianity in large numbers.

Religious historians speculate that the kind of Christianity promoted during this time—emotionally charged, with an emphasis on the personal experience of faith rather than catechetical explanations of it—paralleled in many ways traditional African religion, especially its emphasis of the power of the Holy Spirit to transform the lives of believers. African Americans blended the emotional and experiential elements of the Christianity of the Great Awakening with elements of biblical theology that their white slave owners, for the most part, tried to suppress—namely, God's solidarity with the poor and the oppressed, especially as depicted in the book of Exodus, which tells how God led the Israelites out of bondage in Egypt to freedom in Canaan. White slave owners brought in handpicked ministers and preachers to emphasize and teach those Bible verses that seemed to suggest that God required the obedience of slaves to their masters. Despite these efforts, the biblical theme of the liberation of the enslaved and the poor from bondage was too powerful and too personally applicable for many newly Christianized African slaves to ignore. A number of slave rebellions were inspired by these biblical themes. Among them were the Stono Rebellion in South Carolina (1739), Gabriel's Rebellion in Virginia (1800), and Nat Turner's (1831) also in Virginia, which led a number of southern state legislatures to prohibit reading and writing among slaves.

The fact that African slaves were enthusiastically embracing Christianity led many white Christians, especially in the northern United States, to conclude that slavery was a sin against God. The Religious Society of Friends, a Christian community with roots in the Anabaptist movement and whose members were known as Quakers, was particularly active in the American abolitionist movement, which was devoted to the immediate elimination of slavery in the United States. A key issue for Protestants in favor of abolition was the fact that many slaves had been baptized. They believed that it was a sin for a Christian to own another Christian because baptism connoted the absolute equality of all Christians before the authority and grace of God. Some proslavery Christian leaders, however, asserted that there was no connection to be made between baptism and one's earthly status, as the bishop of London did in this 1727 letter to Christians in the southern colonies:

> **Christianity and the embracing of the gospel does not make the least alteration in Civil property or in any of the duties which belong to civil relations; but in all these respects it continues Persons just in the same State as it found them. The Freedom which Christianity gives is freedom from the Bondage of Sin and Satan and from the Dominion of Men's Lusts and Passions and inordinate Desires; but as to their outward condition, whatever that was before, whether bond or free, their being baptized and becoming Christians, makes no manner of change in them.**

Protestant denominations, with their membership split almost evenly between the northern and southern United States, were placed in the situation of having to weigh the importance of maintaining church unity with the moral demands of the Christian faith, which some people, especially in the North, felt called for an end to slavery. A compromise in many of these denominations, whereby clergy and bishops would speak out against slavery in public without drafting official positions against it in the annual denominational meetings, held these denominations together for a time. However, divergent opinions regarding slavery's compatibility with Christianity caused many denominations to divide into northern and southern factions.

In addition to denominational factionalism by region, American Christianity was divided along racial lines, as well. During the time of the Great Awakening, blacks and whites worshipped together in many American churches, united by their evangelical fervor. This arrangement did not last and blacks were relegated to the balconies of most churches, even in the North, during worship services. The refusal of some black Christians to accept second-class status in church, especially when they were already considered second class in general American society, led to the establishment of all-black Protestant denominations such as the African Methodist Episcopal (A.M.E.) Church in 1816, led by Richard Allen (1760–1831), and the African Methodist Episcopal Zion Church in 1821. With the establishment of these churches, African Americans were in charge for the first time. The churches provided them with places where they could worship in the manner they wished and with platforms from which they could exercise a measure of societal power and influence in American society.

Slavery continued in the United States until 1865, the year the North defeated the South in the American Civil War. Southern states were forced to liberate slaves with the passage of the Thirteenth Amendment. Emancipation, however, did not end the African American struggle for freedom. African Americans in the South were free from formal slavery but were left to fend for themselves with little education, few economic opportunities, and, more often than not, no family structure to depend on for support, as black families had often been sold in piecemeal fashion to different masters living in different regions of the South. For these reasons, African American churches became more valuable than ever to the black community because they served as one of the key centers of support for a newly liberated people when few white institutions would step in to lend assistance.

The black church would prove to be essential to the second major struggle for African American freedom: the civil rights movement. This movement of the 1950s and 1960s sought to eliminate the remaining obstacles to the full participation and equal status under the law for African Americans in American society. The groundwork

Three young girls follow along with the order of worship at a Baptist church in South Carolina.

for this movement was provided by black churches and organizations such as the National Association for the Advancement of Colored People (NAACP). When Rosa Parks refused to give up her seat on the bus to a white man on December 1, 1955, black churches provided a pre-existing base of support for the successful Montgomery Bus Boycott, which was led by the young Baptist minister Martin Luther King Jr.

Historians argue that without the support of the black Protestant churches, the civil rights movement would not have been as successful. Its members provided the movement with the loyal and dedicated foot soldiers who endured beatings by policemen, threats of lynchings by racists, the bombing of their churches by white supremacists, and the murders of their children to win the movement's greatest victories in the passage of a series of federal legislative initiatives: the 1964 Civil Rights Act, which made it illegal for businesses that serve the public to deny service to anyone on the basis of race and barred racial discrimination in the work place; the 1965 Voting Rights Act, which outlawed the practice of making the passing of literacy tests a prerequisite for voting; and the Civil Rights Act of 1968, which sought to end discrimination in the sale and rental of housing.

When King was assassinated while in Memphis, Tennessee, to support a black garbage workers' strike on April 4, 1968, he left a legacy of Christian faith in action and compelling evidence that nonviolence, when practiced on a mass scale, can be an effective weapon against deeply rooted, societal structures of injustice. It can also be claimed that King and his movement embodied the best of the Protestant spirit in their refusal to submit to any earthly or human authority when to do so would cause them to betray the gospel to which they had devoted their lives.

six

THE MODERN ERA

Three main topics provide a sense of the state of protestantism today and the direction in which it appears to be heading. The first concerns the internal Protestant debate about how Christianity should be understood in light of the modern world—developments in modern science and the historical-critical method of biblical interpretation, in particular. The second deals with two issues that Protestantism either has faced or is still facing at present: the ordination of women to the ministry and homosexuality's compatibility with Christian faith. The third concerns the evidence, gathered over the last few decades, indicating that the future center of Protestantism, and Christianity in general, is not to be found on the continents of Europe or North America, but in Asia, Africa, and Latin America.

protestantism and the enlightenment: accommodation and resistance

The conversion of the Roman emperor Constantine (about 275–337) to Christianity in the year 312, effectively made Christianity the official religion of the Roman empire. Since then, Christianity has had few rivals to challenge its dominance in the West. At one time, Islam, which began to make inroads in Europe through the military conquests of the Ottoman empire, presented a serious threat to Christianity's preeminent position. This challenge was felt when the Ottomans extended their territory into southeastern Europe

A rural church stands at the foot of a mountain in Iceland. In the twenty-first century, Protestantism continues to expand its global presence, moving beyond its traditional European and North American base to establish itself more firmly in what is seen as its new frontiers—the continents of Africa, Asia, and South America.

from their base in northern Africa and southwestern Asia after the conquest of Constantinople in 1453. The empire began to decline when European nations to the north began to surpass the Ottomans in military strength.

A second challenge to Christian dominance in the West, one that would displace Christianity from the center of Western intellectual life, was the Enlightenment or the Age of Reason. The ideas of the Enlightenment presented something of a dilemma for Christian leaders and theologians across the denominational spectrum.

In his essay "What Is Enlightenment?" philosopher Immanuel Kant (1724–1804) characterized this movement as follows:

Enlightenment is mankind's exit from its self-incurred immaturity. Immaturity is the inability to make use of one's own understanding without the guidance of another. Self-incurred is this inability if its cause lies not in the lack of understanding but rather in the lack of the resolution and the courage to use it without the guidance of another. *Sapere aude!* Have the courage to use your own understanding! is thus the motto of enlightenment.

One age cannot bind itself, and thus conspire, to place the succeeding age in a situation in which it becomes impossible for it to broaden its knowledge (particularly such pressing knowledge), to cleanse itself of errors, and generally to progress in enlightenment. That would be a crime against human nature, whose original destiny consists in this progress; and posterity would be fully justified to reject these resolutions as concluded in an unauthorized and outrageous manner.

Kant perfectly captures the concerns of the Enlightenment, namely, the promotion of an intellectual stance marked by skepticism about tradition and optimism about the future. The Enlightenment looked down on an uncritical adherence to tradition for tradition's sake. The thinking, enlightened person should always challenge the validity of everything that previous generations had handed down and adopt only what proves to be rational and useful for the present time. This disposition led to a certain optimism among leaders of the Enlightenment because they believed that this rigorous testing of traditional ideas would lead to significant advances in the general state of human society. Enlightenment thinkers argued that the traditions of the past held humanity back from progressing in science, philosophy, and, most importantly, toward the construction of a society free from the frequent warring between Protestants and Catholics and the theological disputes among rival sects within Protantism.

The great social aim of the Enlightenment was to unite humankind behind the goal of establishing a peaceful and harmonious society. This objective was something that religion, with all its divisions and conflicts, Enlightenment thinkers contended, would never be able to accomplish. Instead, they believed that the ideal society would be achieved when human minds were liberated from the authoritarian constraints of past traditions, especially from religious ones, and were guided by reason alone.

In retrospect, the scientific, philosophical, and cultural achievements inspired by the Enlightenment, particularly in the seventeenth and eighteenth centuries, were undeniable. The accomplishments of Isaac Newton (1642–1727) in science, René Descartes (1596–1650) and Kant in philosophy, Jean Jacques Rousseau (1712–1778) and John Locke (1632–1704) in political science, and Adam Smith (1723–1790) and Karl Marx (1818–1883) in economics truly expanded the horizon of human intellectual achievement.

In the world of theology, the spirit of the Enlightenment led a number of theologians to embrace what became known as Deism, a religious outlook characterized by a refusal to accept any theological ideas other than those that could be verified by human reason. This left the Deists with only the broadest and most general of convictions about God. Deism, compared to Christianity, was vague about the specific being and character of God. Deism's lack of specificity on this issue was advantageous in that it afforded Deism the opportunity to unite humankind behind a common theological vision—something that Christianity, Judaism, and Islam were unable to do, according to Deists, because each was grounded in specific cultural histories that prevented them from appealing to anyone outside those particular cultures.

While Deistic ideas provided something of a theological challenge to traditional Christianity, it was in the area of biblical scholarship that the Enlightenment made its most significant impact on modern perceptions of Christianity. Freed from the constraints of tradition, Enlightenment biblical scholars began to study the Christian scriptures as they would any other text, such as Homer's *Odyssey* or William Shakespeare's *Hamlet*. Guided by the Enlightenment's scientific method, which dictated that proper investigations should follow the evidence wherever it led and not be influenced by the bias of the investigator, scholars such as Hermann Samuel Reimarus (1694–1768), Ferdinand Christian Baur (1792–1860), and David Friedrich Strauss (1808–1874) conducted inquiries into what was going on *behind* the biblical text. They hoped to learn who its authors were, which regions and cultures they came from, which ideologies and worldviews they were shaped by, and how the succession of editors and writers had influenced the biblical text's final form. These investigations led some scholars to reject the historical validity of certain biblical miracles and others to suggest that Jesus, the man, was probably different from his portrayal in the New Testament.

In short, Enlightenment biblical scholarship proceeded on the assumption that the Bible was a human document, written by particular persons from particular cultures who had their own histories and ideological biases. While Enlightenment biblical scholars had high regard for the Bible and considered it to be one of the most important documents in Western history, they began to claim that it contained errors, exaggerations, and outdated assumptions about the way the world worked. The idea that God, through the Holy Spirit, somehow played a role in the composition of the Bible was also a proposition these scholars rejected on the grounds that it lay outside the bounds of rational inquiry. Such a thing could neither be objectively proven nor demonstrated but was a matter of faith—something with which the Enlightenment was not concerned as its primary goal was to reach objective conclusions through the judicious weighing of evidence.

protestant responses: Liberal protestantism, fundamentalism, and Neo-orthodoxy

Protestant reactions to the investigations of the Enlightenment were varied and can be grouped into three main categories—those of liberal Protestantism, fundamentalism, and neo-orthodoxy. Liberal Protestants welcomed both the Enlightenment and its work in the areas of theology and biblical studies. In their eyes, the Enlightenment was itself a child of the sixteenth-century Protestant Reformation and was carrying out many of its principles to their logical conclusions. Like the reformers, Enlightenment thinkers stressed the importance of each individual studying the Bible for him or herself. Liberal Protestants also shared with the Enlightenment an optimism that unfettered scientific inquiry would lead to the creation of an ideal society and began to equate this objective with the establishment of what Jesus referred to in the New Testament as the Kingdom of God.

In addition, liberal Protestants believed that God was ultimately the source of all truth, whether it was uncovered in theology, history, or science and, as such, free human inquiry into the origin and development of the Bible was not something to be feared, but welcomed. While some of the miracles in the Bible might be shown to have never occurred, this did not matter much to Protestant liberal theologians like Albrecht Ritschl (1822–1889) and Adolf von Harnack (1851–1930), who believed that the ethical teachings and moral vision of Jesus as presented in the New Testament formed the essence of the Christian religion, not the miracles he was said to have performed nor even whether he was a divine figure. This moral essence, they believed, could never be taken away from Christianity by biblical scholars and could be used, in their minds, to guide and shape the unfolding Enlightenment project itself. From their perspective, the Enlightenment held the key to the future of human civilization and they wanted to align themselves with it to make sure that Protestantism—liberal Protestantism, that is—would be a part of that future.

Another group of Protestants was not as welcoming of the Enlightenment and eventually declared it to be an enemy of Christianity that had to be resisted at all costs. Like the Roman Catholic Church prior to the mid-twentieth century, these Protestants sought to build a wall around Christianity that would protect it from the influence of the Enlightenment. In the eyes of both groups, the Age of Reason was undermining the Christian faith by shaking Christian confidence in the Bible's ability to communicate God's will for humanity, in the authority of the church, and in orthodox Christian doctrine. While Roman Catholicism opted in the First Vatican Council (1869–1870) to expand and strengthen papal authority in response to the Enlightenment, the strategy of these anti-Enlightenment Protestants was to develop the position that would later be known as biblical fundamentalism, a stance that regarded the

Bible to be completely free of all error, even in matters of history and science. Fundamentalists, led by theologians such as Charles Hodge (1797–1878) of Princeton Seminary, maintained that the biblical authors were divinely inspired by God who kept them free from error while their pens were in hand.

One of the most dramatic encounters between Enlightenment rationality and fundamentalism occurred in a Dayton, Tennessee, courtroom in July 1925 when Clarence Darrow and William Jennings Bryan engaged in legal battle over whether Tennessee schools should be allowed to teach the theory of evolution in science courses. The matter would later be referred to as the Scopes Monkey Trial after John Thomas Scopes, who was charged with teaching evolution in his classroom (a violation of Tennessee law at the time), and because of the popular notion that Darwin's theory of evolution meant that human beings and apes shared a common ancestor. Although Bryan technically won the case (Scopes was fined $100), the media, particularly *Baltimore Sun* columnist H. L. Mencken, reported that Darrow had made Bryan look foolish, especially during a cross-examination in which Darrow pressed Bryan on the way certain Bible passages conflicted with the findings of modern science.

While Roman Catholicism would soften its stance somewhat vis-à-vis the Enlightenment in the Second Vatican Council, Protestant fundamentalism refuses to alter its viewpoint and continues as a significant, anti-Enlightenment cultural force within both Protestantism and the general society. Strengthened by North American institutions such as the Moody Bible Institute in Chicago, Dallas Theological Seminary, Jerry Falwell's Liberty University, and Bob Jones University in South Carolina, as well as by the best-selling books of Hal Lindsey (*The Late Great Planet Earth*) and, more recently, Tim LaHaye and Jerry B. Jenkins's *Left Behind* series, fundamentalism persists in its tireless effort to judge what counts as authentic Christianity through what some groups have called its five points: the Bible as inspired and without error; belief in the virgin birth of Jesus; that Jesus, through his death on the cross, endured the punishment that God had reserved for humanity on account of original sin, thus making salvation possible ("satisfaction atonement theory"); belief in Jesus's physical resurrection from the dead; and belief in the miracles of Jesus.

Another Protestant group offered yet a third Protestant response to Enlightenment rationality and formed what became known as the neo-orthodox (new orthodox) movement. Developed by mainly academic theologians and theologically sophisticated Protestant clergy, neo-orthodoxy attempted to navigate a middle road between liberal Protestantism and fundamentalism. Interestingly, many of its leaders, which included theologians Karl Barth (1886–1968) in Europe and Reinhold Niebuhr (1892–1971) in the United States, were at one point committed liberal Protestants. The experience, however, of World War I (1914–1918) caused them to reject Protestant liberalism, specifically its belief in the Enlightenment notion that humanity was steadily progressing morally to the point where Jesus's Kingdom of God would be constructed by human hands on earth. After the deaths of more than ten million men in a war in which new and deadly efficient technologies, such as the machine gun and poison gases, made their infamous military debuts, neo-orthodox theologians believed that the dark side of the Enlightenment was at last revealing itself. When World War II (1939–1945) followed— producing 17 million deaths among soldiers; 6 million systematically exterminated Jews, who were the tragic object of Nazi persecution, along with gypsies, homosexuals, and other "unacceptable" gentiles; and the dropping of two atomic bombs on Hiroshima and Nagasaki, which, combined, killed between 110,000 and 140,000 people—neo-orthodox theologians believed that the Enlightenment and its scientific and technological advances had ultimately proved more death-dealing than life-affirming.

What the liberal Protestants had forgotten, the neo-orthodox believed, were essential biblical teachings about the reality of human sin and the Reformation message that humanity was not the source of its own salvation. The only true source of human hope and optimism was the grace of God offered to humanity through Jesus, which was something one could not find amidst the triumphs and achievements of human civilization. Instead, it could only be given to humanity as a gift by God, who, they maintained, transcended human culture. The neo-orthodox believed that by allowing Protestantism, particularly European Protestantism, to be caught up in Enlightenment culture's fervent faith in human potential, Protestant liberalism lost the capacity to criticize Western culture in key instances, especially in Germany, where many Protestants either participated in Hitler's "final solution" against the Jews or stood by silently while it unfolded.

The neo-orthodox rejected Protestant fundamentalism and its promotion of biblical literalism, as well. They argued that the biblical writers often conveyed God's truth symbolically or poetically, drawing from their culture's particular myths and stories. Others asserted that the Bible was not, in and of itself, the word of God, but only *became* God's word when the Holy Spirit worked in the human heart to make it so. In either case, the Enlightenment's historical-critical approach to the Bible was not seen by the neo-orthodox as a threat to Christianity. The heart of the Christian faith, they argued, was the risen Jesus, who was a reality that transcended mere words on a page. The Bible is authoritative for Christians, the neo-orthodox believed, only because it is the text that bears witness to the reality of Jesus and is not itself this reality. The problem with the fundamentalists, from the perspective of the neo-orthodox, was that they idolatrously worshipped a book, instead of the reality toward which that book pointed.

Neo-orthodox theology, however, was judged by Protestant fundamentalists to be too vague and forceful enough to be accepted as sound Christian theology. For this reason, fundamentalists often make no distinction between liberal Protestants and neo-orthodox Protestants and usually group them together in the "misguided liberal" category. In addition, fundamentalists consider neo-orthodox theological arguments and positions to be too nuanced and sophisticated for many everyday Christians, which is why many Protestants usually identify with either the liberals or the conservative evangelicals or fundamentalists. Neo-orthodox Protestantism, however, stands as an example of an approach that rejects fundamentalism and yet still considers itself evangelical, in maintaining that salvation is only possible through Jesus. What makes its brand of evangelicalism controversial from a conservative evangelical or fundamentalist perspective, is that neo-orthodox theologians often argue that salvation in Jesus is not limited to Christians, but encompasses all of creation, Christians and non-Christians alike.

Two issues of Debate in contemporary protestantism

As the twentieth century continued to unfold, a number of issues provoked considerable debate among estern Protestants that further widened the divide between its conservative and liberal wings. These two issues pertain to gender and sexual orientation.

The Ordination of Women

Of the three main branches of Christianity (Roman Catholicism, Eastern Orthodoxy, and Protestantism), the only churches that ordain women clergy are found within the Protestant fold. For those Protestant Christians who believe in the full equality of women within the church, this fact is a source of tremendous pride. This does not mean that Protestantism was especially progressive on this issue in comparison to mainstream Western society. As Rosemary Keller has observed, although women gained the right to vote in the United States in 1920, the Methodist Church did not begin to ordain women until 1956. The Methodist and Presbyterian churches were among the first mainline Protestant denominations to do so, with mainline Lutheranism resolving to ordain women in 1970 and the Episcopal Church in 1976.

The role of women in the church remains a topic of debate within some Protestant circles, especially in conservative evangelical and fundamentalist Protestant communities. Those who are opposed to the practice of ordaining women usually argue that it runs contrary to scripture and cite such biblical passages as Genesis 2:18–23, in which Eve is described as Adam's "helper," 1 Corinthians 11:3–15, where Paul writes that the male "is the image and reflection of God; but woman is the reflection of man," and 1 Corinthians 14:34–35:

> **. . . women should be silent in the churches. For they are not permitted to speak, but should be subordinate, as the law also says. If there is anything they desire to know, let them ask their husbands at home. For it is shameful for a woman to speak in church.**

Proponents of women's ordination also quote scripture in support of their position, including Genesis 1:26–31, in which it is suggested

The traditional notion of a male spiritual leader has altered over the past half century as some branches of Protestantism welcomed female pastors and ministers into the fold. No matter who is at the helm of a congregation, translating the faith's message to the next generation of followers stands at the forefront of the many challenges Protestant sects face in the twenty-first century.

that men and women together constitute the one image of God, and Galatians 3:27–28, where Paul writes that among the baptized distinctions of ethnicity, civil status, and gender no longer pertain:

> . . . for in Christ Jesus you are all children of God through faith. As many of you as were baptized into Christ have clothed yourselves with Christ. There is no longer Jew or Greek, there is no longer slave or free, there is no longer male and female; for all of you are one in Christ Jesus.

As a result of lifting the ban on women's ordination, women have steadily risen to positions of influence and authority within the Protestant denominations that chose to adopt that course. In the United Methodist Church, for example, eleven of the fifty-three bishops were, as of 2005, women, with women also constituting

43 percent of the delegates at the denomination's 2004 General Conference, its main meeting of United Methodist leaders. Statistics from the North American Association of Theological Schools also reveal that 35 percent of Protestant seminarians in 2004 were women, compared with 10 percent in 1972. No doubt these figures will increase as Protestants become increasingly acclimated to the ministerial leadership of women in their churches and especially if conservative denominations reconsider their objections to the ordination of women in the twenty-first century.

Homosexuality

Another topic of debate within contemporary Protestantism concerns the compatibility of homosexuality with Christian faith. This issue threatens to divide many Protestant denominations, with one side believing that the two are incompatible and the other asserting the contrary. Until the latter half of the twentieth century, this particular issue was seldom discussed in denominational gatherings, as the consensus in both mainstream society and in Christian churches was that homosexuality was an abnormality, a deviation from accepted human behavior. This changed, especially in Europe and North America, with the emergence of the gay pride movement, which encouraged homosexuals to reject the notion that they were somehow "abnormal" or "deviant" and to "come out" or refuse to keep their homosexuality a secret from their families, friends, and acquaintances. Another major factor was the 1973 decision by the American Psychiatric Association to remove homosexuality from its list of common psychological disorders. As a consequence, some denominations reconsidered their classification of homosexuality as a sin.

In addition, modern historical-critical biblical scholarship has brought forth theories and hypotheses that have caused some to read the biblical passages commonly used to condemn homosexual practice in a different light. To take one example, some scholars contend that what many have taken to be Paul's explicit, unambiguous condemnation of homosexuality in Romans 1:26–27 and 1 Corinthians 6:9 was, in and for Paul's time, a condemnation of pederasty and slave prostitution involving older men and young boys—something qualitatively different from a mutual and consenting relationship between two responsible adults of the same sex. Such theories, however, are often unpersuasive to Protestant fundamentalists and conservative evangelicals who reject the validity of the historical-critical method of biblical scholarship altogether and focus instead on the "plain sense" of the text, an interpretive approach that makes no distinction between the way biblical passages were understood in their original context and the way that they are now viewed.

Protestants opposed to homosexuality also view its acceptance in some, mostly liberal Protestant circles as a symptom of contemporary Protestantism's failure to stand firm on basic moral and theological principles amidst the shifting tides of contemporary Western culture. They argue that the slide into extreme individualism and moral relativism is something that the church should be fighting, not accommodating. But whether Protestant acceptance of homosexuality represents a failure of nerve to stand firm on traditional Christian teachings or is in keeping with the spirit of Protestantism insofar as it represents both a refusal to follow tradition for tradition's sake and a protest against those who would place limits on God's grace, this issue will no doubt continue to be passionately debated and discussed within Protestant denominations for the foreseeable future.

globalization and protestantism: asia, africa, and latin america

During the latter half of the twentieth century, statistical research into global church membership, mostly compiled by David B.

Barrett, George T. Kurian, and Todd Johnson in their influential *World Christian Encyclopedia*, suggested that Asia, Africa, and Latin America will displace North American and Europe from their position as the controlling center of both Protestantism and Christianity. In his summary of a report based on those findings issued by Barrett and Johnson, Allan Anderson wrote the following:

> At the beginning of the twentieth century, there were an estimated 90 million Christians in Asia, Africa and Latin America, 16 per cent of the world's Christian population, compared to 428 million or 77 per cent in Europe (including Russia) and North America. A century later, according to Barrett and Johnson's statistics, there were 1,118 million Christians in Asia, Africa and Latin America, 59 per cent of the world's Christians, while those of the two northern continents [Europe and North America] only constituted 39 per cent. Barrett and Johnson's statistics give dramatic evidence of how rapidly the "Western" share of world Christianity decreased in the twentieth century. The demographic balance of Christianity has been shifting steadily southwards. They estimate that if present trends continue, 68 per cent of the world's Christians will live in the South by 2025, with only 31 per cent in the North.

These statistics are usually very surprising to European and North American Christians, and function as a kind of "reality check" against unspoken assumptions about Christianity being primarily a Western religion. A quick study of early Christian history reveals that Christianity technically began in western Asia and was well established in north Africa during Christianity's first four centuries, which challenges the common association of Christian with Western.

History also makes clear that, whatever its origins, Christianity migrated and became firmly established in the Western world from the time of Constantine's conversion onward. It was also Western Protestant and Catholic missionaries who helped to pave the way for Christianity to become a significant part of the contemporary religious landscape in Asia, Africa, and Latin America.

During Protestantism's first centuries, Europe was the main focus of its evangelistic outreach, as Lutheranism and Calvinism vigorously competed with Roman Catholicism to win converts among the continent's rulers and citizens. During the time of the Enlightenment, Protestantism began to extend its reach into other parts of the world. For this reason, there is some debate among historians as to whether the Protestant missions of this time were more reflective of the spirit of the Enlightenment than the spirit of Luther and Calvin. Both Luther and Calvin, for instance, believed that one's acceptance of the gospel of Jesus was a matter determined ultimately by the Holy Spirit and was not a matter of human choice; it pertained exclusively to God's hidden, providential plan.

With the rise of Pietism, which did much to popularize Arminian Protestantism and its teaching that human beings had to make a free conscious decision to accept the gospel in order to be "saved," Protestant ideas of election and predestination began to be pushed aside—a tendency to which the Enlightenment's emphasis on individual freedom and responsibility contributed as well. As this shift in theology occurred at the same time as European ventures into the lands and cultures beyond the West began in earnest, all the conditions were in place for the modern Protestant missionary movement to come into its own. If salvation was a matter of human decision, not divine election, then the missionaries believed that as Christians they had a moral obligation to bring the gospel to the places in the world that had not yet heard it, for the eternal destiny of untold numbers of human souls was at stake.

Some Christian theologians, historians, and, in particular, Asian, African, and Latin American intellectuals whose cultures were made the focus of Protestant missions during the Enlightenment era criticize the early missionaries for their failure to distinguish between the gospel of Jesus and European culture. In many instances, the two were held to be virtually synonymous: Asian, African, and Latin American persons who converted to Christianity were also often pressured or even forced to abandon their own cultural practices and customs and adopt ill-fitting European ones—just as many Native Americans were forced to do by Christians of European origin in North America. For this reason, during the period of European colonial expansion, whose time roughly extended from initial Portuguese ventures into Africa in the 1400s to the middle of the twentieth century, European colonizers found Christian missionaries of great use as they helped "Europeanize" the indigenous persons in those regions, making them more likely to cooperate with the colonization process. In those years, European nations took control of large portions of Asia, Africa, and Latin America and greatly expanded European wealth and power by profiting from the natural resources and the cheap—sometimes slave—labor of those regions.

One of the consequences of the Christian mission movement was that the educational system it established in areas of Asia, Africa, and Latin America produced, contrary to the intent of European colonizers, many of the leaders of the later independence movements against colonial forces, such as Mohandas Gandhi who led successful resistance to British rule in India in the first half of the twentieth century. As this new independent, nationalist spirit among once colonized peoples began to spread after World War II, many of the churches established by Western Protestants came under heavy suspicion, viewed as lingering agents of European colonialism. By 1971 Western missionary activity was suspended by many Protestant church authorities in the Philippines, Kenya, and Argentina—a symbolic end, perhaps, to mainline Protestant involvement in foreign missions.

pentecostalism: the future of global christianity?

Yet, Barrett and Johnson's research points to the rapid growth of Protestant Christianity in Asia, Africa, and Latin America. This is mostly due not to the efforts of traditional, mainline Protestantism but to the spread of Pentecostal Christianity throughout the world. Barrett and Johnson's research indicates that, in 2002, more than 543 million Christians in the world identified themselves with some variety of Pentecostalism, which would constitute approximately 26 percent of the world Christian population—second only to Roman Catholicism in terms of total, worldwide membership among Christians. Scholars debate whether Pentecostalism should be classified as a Protestant movement, as its practice of Christianity is different from that of many traditional denominations. Research has shown, however, that Pentecostalism's roots can be traced to the Protestant evangelical revivalism of the nineteenth century, which serves as a good argument for its inclusion in the Protestant fold.

Pentecostalism's defining features include the individual believer's direct and personal experience of the Holy Spirit, which often manifests itself in ecstatic and emotional demonstrations during Pentecostal worship services. These demonstrations sometimes take the form of what is referred to as speaking in tongues, which occurs, according to Pentecostals, when an individual is seized by the Holy Spirit and begins speaking in different languages, just as the disciples were reported to have done in the second chapter of the New Testament book of Acts.

The Pentecostal movement continues to gain force and momentum on the world stage, drawing ever-growing legions of followers particularly in Central and South America. Asia and sub-Saharan Africa have also seen an explosion in the number of Pentecostal members in recent years. Its appeal lies in its ability to adapt itself to and to integrate established local customs and traditions.

Pentecostalism is believed to have become a distinct Christian movement and not merely a footnote to Protestant revivalist evangelicalism, in 1906, the year of the Azusa Street revival in Los Angeles. The African American pastor and son of freed slaves William Joseph Seymour began leading prayer services in homes on Azusa Street after he was forced out as pastor of a Wesleyan Holiness Church, which objected to his belief that authentic Christianity required speaking in tongues. Members of that church who supported Seymour began attending the home prayer services where they witnessed what they believed were unmistakable signs of the inbreaking of the Holy Spirit, including speaking in tongues and persons collapsing and falling unconscious as Seymour laid his hands on them. Word spread about Seymour's prayer meetings on Azusa Street. Over the next three years, people from all over the world came to observe for themselves what many believed to be the restoration of the original Christianity of the apostles—a sign for many that the second coming, or return of Jesus, was imminent.

With Azusa Street as its epicenter, the Pentecostal movement spread throughout the globe. In the United States, the largest denomination that traces its origins to Azusa Street is the Assemblies of God, whose members include former U.S. Attorney General John Ashcroft—a strong indicator that Pentecostalism is making significant inroads into mainstream American society. In 2004, 10 percent of Latin America was reported to be broadly Pentecostal, including 30 percent of Guatemala and 20 percent of both Brazil and Chile. If present trends persist in Asia and sub-Saharan Africa, Pentecostalism will dwarf all other forms of Christianity, as it continues to grow in countries such as China, South Korea, the Philippines, Indonesia, India, Ghana, Nigeria, and South Africa. One of Pentecostalism's great advantages in winning cross-cultural acceptance is its ability to adapt itself to local traditions and worldviews. This has the reported effect of making non-Western practitioners of Pentecostalism feel as if they are practicing a form of Christianity that is truly theirs, not one that is imposed upon them from the outside.

Some scholars, such as Harvey Cox of Harvard University, have argued that these Pentecostal movements, in subsequent generations, begin to lose their flexibility and fluidity and adopt, over time, comparatively more fixed, even fundamentalist, theological principles. Whether this is the case remains to be observed as Protestantism moves ahead into the twenty-first century—its sixth century as a major, and now global, expression of the Christian religion.

TIME LINE

1517
Martin Luther nails his Ninety-five Theses to the door of the church at Wittenburg.

1520
Pope Leo X issues the bull *Exsurge Domine*, which threatens to excommunicate Martin Luther.

1521
Luther appears before representatives of the Holy Roman Empire at Worms (April 17–18).

1524–1525
The Peasants' War, the greatest mass uprising in German history, takes place, inspired to a large extent by Luther's theology. Luther refuses to support the uprising and sides with the established authorities against the peasants.

1534
Henry VIII declares himself supreme head of the English Church.

1536
John Calvin arrives in Geneva. The first edition of the *Institutes of the Christian Religion* is published in Latin.

1618–1619
The Synod of Dort, an assembly of the Dutch Reformed Church, convenes to refute Arminianism.

1620
Puritans settle in Massachusetts and begin to set up the Congregational Church.

1641
Earliest recorded baptism of an African slave takes place in Massachusetts.

1689
The Act of Toleration is passed by the English Parliament. It grants religious freedom to Protestants not affiliated with the Anglican Church, but not to Roman Catholics or Jews.

1738
John Wesley's heart is "warmed" while hearing Luther's preface to the Letter to the Romans read at a religious service on Aldersgate Street in London.

1739
George Whitefield's preaching tour of the American colonies ignites the Great Awakening.

1784
Immanuel Kant publishes his essay, "What Is Enlightenment?"

1816
Richard Allen founds the African Methodist Episcopal (A.M.E.) Church.

1835
David Friedrich Strauss's *Life of Jesus*, which disputes the historicity of certain aspects of the New Testament, is published.

1845
Southern Baptists break from the national Baptist organization.

1906
Azusa Street gatherings commence, marking the beginning of
Pentecostalism.

1910
The Presbyterian Church passes the "Five Point Defense," a
statement outlining the essential doctrines to which a Christian
fundamentalist must adhere.

1918
The first edition of Karl Barth's *The Letter to the Romans,* a
founding text of the neo-orthodoxy movement, is published.

1922
Harry Emerson Fosdick preaches his sermon "Shall the
Fundamentalists Win?" from the pulpit of the First Presbyterian
Church in New York City.

1925
The Scopes Monkey Trial takes place in a Dayton, Tennessee,
courtroom.

1949
Evangelist Billy Graham holds his first of many "crusades" before
mass audiences in Los Angeles.

1956
The Methodist Church lifts its ban on the ordination of women.

1961
Televangelist Pat Robertson's Christian Broadcast Network (CBN)
begins broadcasting on a UHF channel in Portsmouth, Virginia.

1964
The Civil Rights Act of 1964 is passed, which bans discrimination

because of a person's color, race, national origin, religion, or sex in the United States.

1971
Western missionary activity is suspended by many Protestant church authorities in the Philippines, Kenya, and Argentina.

2003
The Right Reverend V. Gene Robinson, an openly gay man, is consecrated as bishop of the Diocese of New Hampshire in the Episcopal Church.

GLOSSARY

antinomianism—The name for the view that those who are saved by God's grace no longer need to follow moral and ethical guidelines.

Arminianism—The theological movement that opposes the view that God elects or predestines those who will be saved in Jesus. It maintains that human beings are given the freedom to accept or reject God's offer of salvation through Jesus.

baptism—The sacrament through which one is inducted into the church, either through immersion (full submersion in water) or affusion (the pouring or sprinkling of water over one's head).

believer's baptism—A baptism that is preceded by, and conditional upon, a public profession of faith on the part of the baptismal candidate.

decretum horribile—The "horrible decree." In Calvin's theology it was used to describe the teaching that God predestines some to spend eternity in hell.

deism—The theological position which holds that the propositions "God exists" and "God is the creator of the universe" can be derived strictly from an observation of the natural world. Its adherents, known as Deists, also believe that God is not involved in the ongoing affairs of the world, but lets the world run its course without interference or intervention.

election—In Calvinist theology, the act by which God predestines individuals for salvation.

The Enlightenment (Age of Reason)—The period in Europe, usually associated with the eighteenth century, in which the primary authority over intellectual and scientific matters switched from faith and scripture to reason and the scientific method.

Eucharist (Lord's Supper)—A sacrament and the central act of worship in most Christian communities in which those gathered reenact Jesus and his disciples' Last Supper by sharing a meal of bread and wine. Theological disputes have centered on the extent to which Jesus is thought to be present in the Eucharistic bread and wine, as well as the manner in which the sacrament takes place.

evangelicalism—Initially, the term *evangelical* was used to describe those who associated themselves with the Protestant Reformation. In the modern era, the term is associated with forms of Christianity which hold that salvation is predicated on one making a personal decision to accept Jesus as one's personal savior. Accordingly, the importance of sharing the good news gospel with non-Christians in the hope that they will convert to the Christian faith is often emphasized.

Exsurge Domine—The bull issued by Pope Leo X, dated June 15, 1520, threatening to excommunicate Martin Luther from the Roman Catholic Church. In defiant response, Luther publicly burned the document at Wittenburg on December 10, 1520.

fundamentalism—A cross-denominational movement that arrived on the American scene after World War I (1914–1918) to oppose the theory of evolution and the historical critical method of biblical interpretation. The five points of Christian fundamentalism have traditionally been belief in the inerrancy of the Bible, the divinity of Jesus, the Virgin Birth of Jesus, the substitutionary theory of the Atonement, and the bodily return of Jesus at the second coming.

gospel—The central content of what Christians believe is God's revelation to the world, namely the good news that God has reconciled the world to God's self through the person of Jesus. It is also used to refer to the four New Testament books in which this good news is reported: Matthew, Mark, Luke, and John.

grace—The supernatural assistance that God gives to human beings so that they may know God and do God's work on earth. Christians believe that grace brings one to faith in Jesus and afterward nurtures and sustains that faith.

Great Awakening—The period of intense religiosity that took the American colonies by storm during the mid1700s. It was sparked by dynamic preaching that dramatically emphasized the individual's direct and personal experience of God in the person of Jesus.

historical-critical method of biblical interpretation—An approach to the study of the Bible that attempts to understand biblical passages in light of their authors' and editors' political, historical, and sociological contexts.

Holy Spirit—The third person of the Trinity, according to Christian doctrine. Calvin believed that one of its functions was to render the Bible revelatory, or disclose God's self, to the reader.

hymn—A song sung in Christian worship services whose lyrics explain Christian doctrine, explore the life of faith, or recount biblical events.

indulgences—Acts thought to remit the punishment of human sin. Indignation over their sale prompted Martin Luther to question the authority of the Roman Catholic hierarchy in the sixteenth century.

invisible church—The notion, usually attributed to John Calvin, that within the visible structure of the church there exists a hidden church of the elect known only to God.

justification by faith alone—The Protestant teaching that God reconciles human beings to God's self, following the breach caused by original sin, unconditionally, or without respect to whether they deserve or have earned that privilege.

Kingdom of God—A central element in Jesus's teaching that concerns the establishment of a divinely instituted reign of justice that encompasses the entire creation. It is presented in the New Testament as both a present and a future reality.

law and gospel—The traditional structure of Lutheran preaching in which the recognition of the human difficulty in living up to the high standards of biblical law is juxtaposed with the gospel message that one is justified by faith, not by works.

liberal Protestantism—The movement within Protestantism that believes that Christianity must adapt its message to comport well with the modern world ushered in by the Enlightenment. Liberal Protestants often incorporate the latest findings of science, philosophy, psychology, and the historical-critical method of biblical interpretation into their theology.

Mass—A service of worship, usually associated with Roman Catholic congregations, that consists of two main parts: (1) the reading of scripture and the preaching of a sermon or homily, and (2) the celebration of the Eucharist.

neo-orthodoxy—A non-fundamentalist evangelical Protestant movement, composed mostly of academic theologians, that arose to oppose liberal Protestantism after the First World War. What neo-orthodox theologians found objectionable about liberal Protestantism was its emphasis upon reason and human experience, as opposed to faith and divine revelation. Their rejection of biblical inerrancy and support of universalism placed them at odds with many fundamentalists.

Ninety-five Theses—The document that Luther, on October 31, 1517, nailed to the door of the castle church at Wittenburg in order to condemn the practice of indulgence sales. The Ninety-five Theses became a popular manifesto for church reform and led to Luther's break from the Roman Catholic Church.

original sin—In classical Christianity, humanity's fundamental condition following the Fall of Adam and Eve in the Garden of Eden, that is, as existing in a state of estrangement or alienation from God. Salvation, in Christian theology, is the act or process, by which this condition is corrected.

Peasants' War—A bloody rebellion that took place in 1524 and 1525, in which German peasants rose up against feudal lords. Martin Luther's view that the Bible was the sole authority for the Christian, not human authorities, was cited by the peasants to justify their actions. Luther refused to back the rebellion and declared his support for the rebellion's violent suppression at the hands of the governing authorities. In the end, as many as 100,000 peasants lost their lives.

predestination—The idea that before the creation of the world God had knowledge of all events that would transpire, from the smallest to the most significant detail. In Protestant theology, is the idea that God knows in advance who will be saved in Jesus. Double predestination names that view, held by John Calvin, that God has earmarked some people for salvation and others for damnation.

priesthood of all believers—A principle that holds that there is no distinction, in the eyes of God, between the clergy and the laity, as those who have been restored to right relationship with God through faith have done so as a result of God's grace, not by way of their own moral purity or righteousness.

Puritanism—An English Protestant movement that strove to purify the church by limiting it to those whose Christian faith was judged to be authentic. The movement came to the American colonies during the seventeenth century, when those Puritans dissatisfied with the Church of England attempted to establish in North America the purified Christian communities for which they longed.

Radical Reformation—The name given to the sixteenth-century Protestant movement that sought to take the Reformation far beyond what Luther and Calvin thought prudent. They argued for the complete separation of church and state and advocated what became known as believer's baptism. The Anabaptists, Mennonites, and the Amish were some of this movement's earliest representatives.

sacrament—Defined in the English Book of Common Prayer as "an outward and visible sign of an inward and spiritual grace." Protestants, generally speaking, recognize the Eucharist and baptism as authentic sacraments, while Roman Catholics count seven sacraments: the Eucharist, baptism, confirmation, penance, extreme unction, holy orders, and holy matrimony.

sermon—A discourse delivered in the context of Christian worship that seeks to interpret or expound upon selected biblical texts.

Simul iustus et simul peccator—The Latin expression meaning "at the same time both righteous and a sinner." For Luther, it described the state of the individual following his or her justification by faith alone: Because such a person possessed no innate righteousness, in and of his or herself, that person was still considered to be a sinner. At the same time, this same sinner was considered righteous because of God's decision not to count this against him or her.

sola scriptura—The Latin expression meaning "scripture alone." This was a fundamental theological principle for the Protestant Reformation as it expressed the principle that the Bible, not the pope, was the supreme authority in the life of the Christian.

televangelism—The term used in the latter half of the twentieth century to describe the practice of spreading the Christian gospel through television broadcasting. Televangelism's origins can be traced to October 1, 1961, the date that evangelist Pat Robertson's Christian Broadcast Network (CBN) went on the air on a UHF channel in Portsmouth, Virginia. By 2006 CBN was broadcasting to approximately 200 countries.

Thirty Years' War—A war, lasting from 1618 to 1648, that began as a civil war between Protestants and Catholics within the Holy Roman empire and spilled over into most of Europe. On October 24, 1648, the Peace of Westphalia was signed, bringing the war to its conclusion.

two kingdoms theory—Luther's understanding of the way the spiritual kingdom of God related to the worldly kingdoms governed by human authorities. In the spiritual kingdom, God rules through the gospel of Jesus, while in the worldly one, God rules through the established, human governing authorities.

universalism—In Christian theology, the notion that no one will be excluded from God's offer of salvation through Jesus, including those who are not explicit practitioners of Christianity.

Wesleyan Quadrilateral—The Methodist principle which states that the essentials of the Christian faith are determined on the basis of scripture, tradition, reason, and experience.

FURTHER RESOURCES

American Sermons: The Pilgrims to Martin Luther King, Jr. New York: The Library of America, 1999.

Bainton, Roland. *Here I Stand: A Life of Martin Luther.* New York: Abingdon-Cokebury Press, 1950.

Barrett, David B., George T. Kurian, and Todd M. Johnson, eds. *World Christian Encyclopedia.* New York: Oxford University Press, 2001.

Braaten, Carl E. and Robert W. Jenson, eds. *A Map of Twentieth Century Theology.* Minneapolis: Fortress Press, 1995.

Bowie, Walter Russell and Kenneth Seeman Giniger, eds. *What Is Protestantism?* New York: Franklin Watts, 1965.

Brown, Robert McAfee. *The Spirit of Protestantism.* New York: Oxford University Press, 1961.

Calvin, John. *Calvin's Institutes: A New Compendium.* ed. Hugh T. Kerr. Louisville, KY: Westminster/John Knox Press, 1989.

———. *Institutes of the Christian Religion.* ed. John T. McNeill, trans. Ford Lewis Battles. Philadelphia: Westminster Press, 1960.

Cox, Harvey. *Fire from Heaven: The Rise of Pentecostal Spirituality and the Reshaping of Religion in the Twenty-first Century.* Reading, MA: Addison-Wesley, 1995.

Cross, F. L. and E. A. Livingstone, eds. *The Oxford Dictionary of the Christian Church.* New York: Oxford University Press, 2005.

Douglas, J. D., Walter A. Elwell, and Peter Toon, eds. *The Concise Dictionary of the Christian Tradition.* Grand Rapids, MI: Regency Reference Library, 1989.

González, Justo L. *The Story of Christianity.* Vol. 2, The Reformation to the Present Day. San Francisco: Harper and Row, 1984.

Hillerbrand, Hans J., ed. *The Encyclopedia of Protestantism.* New York: Routledge, 2004.

Lindner, Eileen W., ed. *Yearbook of American & Canadian Churches 2005.* Nashville: Abingdon Press, 2005.

Luther, Martin. *Martin Luther's Basic Theological Writings.* ed. Timothy F. Lull. Minneapolis: Fortress Press, 1989.

————. *Martin Luther: Selections from his Writings.* ed. John Dillenberger. Garden City, NY: Doubleday, 1961.

Marty, Martin E. *Protestantism.* New York: Holt, Rinehart and Winston, 1972.

McCue, James F. "Luther and Roman Catholicism on the Mass as Sacrifice," in *The Eucharist as Sacrifice.* New York: U.S.A. National Committee of the Lutheran World Federation, 1968.

McGrath, Alister E. and Darren C. Marks, eds. *The Blackwell Companion to Protestantism.* Malden, MA: Blackwell Publishing, 2004.

Morse, Christopher. *Not Every Spirit: A Dogmatics of Christian Disbelief.* Valley Forge, PA: Trinity Press International, 1994.

Musser, Donald W. and Joseph L. Price, eds. *A New Handbook of Christian Theology.* Nashville: Abingdon Press, 1992.

Niebuhr, Reinhold. *Moral Man and Immoral Society.* Louisville, KY: Westminster John Knox Press, 2001.

Pelikan, Jaroslav. *The Christian Tradition: A History of the Development of Doctrine*. Vol. 4, *Reformation of Church and Dogma (1300–1700)*. Chicago: University of Chicago Press, 1984.

Placher, William C. *A History of Christian Theology: An Introduction*. Philadelphia: Westminster Press, 1983.

Ritschl, Albrecht. *Albrecht Ritschl: Three Essays*, trans. Philip Hefner. Philadelphia: Fortress Press, 1972.

Schmidt, James, ed. *What Is Enlightenment? Eighteenth-Century Answers and Twentieth-Century Questions*. Berkeley: University of California Press, 1996.

SOURCE NOTES

All biblical quotations are taken from the New Revised Standard Version.

CHAPTER ONE:

p. 13: "It is not against all natural reason that . . .": Roland Bainton, *Here I Stand: A Life of Martin Luther*. (New York: Abingdon Press, 1950), p. 45.

p. 16: "Though I lived as a monk without reproach . . .": Martin Luther, "Preface to Latin Writings," in *Martin Luther: Selections from His Writings*, ed. John Dillenberger (New York: Doubleday, 1961), p. 11.

pp. 20–21: "43. Christians are to be taught that . . .": Martin Luther, "The Ninety-five Theses (1517)," from *Martin Luther's Basic Theological Writings*, ed. Timothy F. Lull (Minneapolis: Fortress Press, 1989), pp. 21–29.

p. 23: "Unless I am convicted by Scripture . . .": Bainton, *Here I Stand*, p. 185.

p. 23: "Luther is to be regarded as a convicted heretic. . . .": Bainton, *Here I Stand*, p. 189.

CHAPTER TWO:

pp. 28–29 : "Since for believing men religion seems . . .": John Calvin, *Calvin's Institutes: A New Compendium*, ed. Hugh T. Kerr (Louisville: Westminster/John Knox Press, 1989), p. 31.

p. 32: "Although the Christian is thus free . . .": Martin Luther, "The Freedom of a Christian," in *Martin Luther: Selections from His Writings*, ed. John Dillenberger (New York: Doubleday, 1961), p. 75.

pp. 32–33: "Our faith in Christ does not free us from works . . .": Luther, *Selections from His Writings*, p. 81

pp. 33–34: "I frankly confess that, for myself, . . . :" Luther, *Selections from his Writings*, p. 199.

pp. 35–37: "In actual fact, the covenant of life . . .": John Calvin, *Institutes of the Christian Religion*, ed. John T. McNeill, trans. Ford Lewis Battles (Philadelphia: Westminster Press, 1960), pp. 920–921.

p. 39: ". . . to embrace the unity of the church in this way, . . .": Calvin, *Institutes*, p. 1015.

p. 39: "For as we know not who belongs . . .": Calvin, *Institutes*, p. 964.

p. 40: "it is not to be doubted, a church of God exists.": Kerr, *Calvin's Institutes*, p. 133.

CHAPTER FOUR:

p. 71: ". . . it is not enough or in any sense Christian . . .": Martin Luther, "The Freedom of the Christian," in Dillenberger, pp. 65–66.

p. 72: "Those whose authority of the Word . . .": Calvin, *Institutes*, p. 1018.

CHAPTER FIVE:

p. 82: "Those two things are quite contrary: . . .": Luther, "Commentary on Galatians," in Dillenberger, pp. 132–133.

p. 83: "If we share in his resurrection, through it . . .": Calvin, *Institutes*, p. 601.

pp. 89–90: "The social gospel is the old message of salvation, . . .": Walter Rauschenbusch, "Theology and the Social Gospel," in *A Map of Twentieth Century Theology*, eds. Carl E. Braaten and Robert W. Jenson (Minneapolis: Fortress Press, 1995), pp. 356–357.

p. 93: "Christianity and the embracing of the gospel does not make.": Quoted by Reinhold Niebuhr, *Moral Man and Immoral Society.* (Louisville, KY: Westminster/John Knox Press, 2001), p. 78.

CHAPTER SIX:

p. 99: "Enlightenment is mankind's exit from its self-incurred immaturity.": Immanuel Kant, "An Answer to the Question: What Is Enlightenment?" in *What Is Enlightenment? Eighteenth-Century Answers and Twentieth-Century Questions*, ed. James Schmidt (Berkeley: University of California Press, 1996), p. 58.

INDEX
Page numbers in boldface are illustrations.

ABOUT THE AUTHOR

A 1995 graduate of Saint Olaf College and a lay member of the United Methodist Church, Trevor Eppehimer earned a Master of Divinity (MDiv) degree from Yale Divinity School (1999) and a Doctor of Philosophy (PhD) from Union Theological Seminary in New York (2006). He is a former editor of the *Union Seminary Quarterly Review* and is currently a lecturer in theology and philosophy of religion at Union Theological Seminary in New York, where he lives with his wife, Victoria, and their daughter, Grace.